Times in the
Life of a Seattle Icon

John Pierre

CLASSIC DAY
PUBLISHING

Seattle, Washington
Portland, Oregon
Denver, Colorado
Vancouver, B.C.
Scottsdale, Arizona
Minneapolis, Minnesota

Classic Day Publishing
Houseboat #4
2207 Fairview Avenue East
Seattle, Washington 98102
877-728-8837
ewolfpub@aol.com

CONTENTS

ACKNOWLEDGMENTS

There are many who have contributed in one way or another to this story of Joe Diamond's life … so far. Far too many have offered unselfishly of their time and input for me even to attempt to name all without unforgivable omissions.

I could begin by acknowledging the friends and associates of Joe Diamond who were kind enough to share their thoughts with readers of Joe's "Book of Memories" presented to him on the occasion of his 83rd birthday. There were over 200 such contributors, and it was my unfortunate duty to have to select from their heartfelt comments for presentation here.

Most important to this writing, however, is Josef Diamond himself. His encouragement has been the most important piece to the project. Since I first met him nearly 44 years ago, he has continued to encourage me to write and has given me confidence in my ability to do so. He has spent numerous hours with me on this specific effort to make absolutely sure that everything has been related as honestly and error free as possible. The only liberty taken with the facts is my use of some fictitious names to protect the identity of some of the subjects of the tales.

Equally important to this undertaking is Muriel Bach Diamond—Joe's beautiful and talented wife of nearly 20 years. It is hard to adequately express the appreciation I feel for Muriel. She has been a consistent supporter and has lent her strength and reassurance in every aspect of the several months of preparation.

There are others who have meant so much: Joel Diamond (Joe's son); Jerry Alhadeff (Joe's partner in many ventures); Somers White, who was as much of an instigator to get this writing under way as Josef and Muriel were. Norm Ginsberg has been of immeasurable assistance throughout the production of this volume.

Judy Ann Moulton has been of great help in correcting my numerous typos and my frequently improper punctuation, as well as providing a special knowledge of the history of a man she and I both adore—Joe Diamond.

Then there is a very important person to this conglomeration of nouns and verbs: Elliott Wolf, our publisher. Elliott is more than just a publisher and employer of cover artists, designers, and an editor; he has become a friend.

And last (not that she shouldn't be first) is my good wife of 52 years, Rosie. She put up with me working in the middle of the night, banging away on the computer keyboard, flipping through the thesaurus and dictionary, and missed a few dinner appointments and other indignities because, like me, she thought Joe Diamond's story was worth telling.

To all of these and any others I might have temporarily overlooked, you have my thanks.

In Loving Memory

RUBY AND MICHAEL DIAMOND

FOREWORD

For the last 19 years I've been trying to get to know this man, Joe Diamond, who has been a loving, loyal, lovable husband but not one who reveals himself easily.

With this publication, I have an opportunity to know what he was up to those 78 years when he was unknown to me. I expect nothing will surprise me because I have found him daring, at times hardheaded and occasionally blind to reality yet always patient and determined not to hurt feelings—quite a feat for a stubborn soul with a delightful sense of humor.

However, it didn't take 19 years to discover he has a mania for perfection. Even at the age of six he refused to go to school because of a button missing from his shirt. His attitudes toward loyalty are unshakable, possibly because he has perfected the art of forgetting what he doesn't want to remember. He is what he is.

I've often wondered what it was that drew the two of us so very different people together in a remarkably short time. Our tastes, our backgrounds, our interests are all very different but for one thing. We each have an insatiable need to love and be loved. This we found in each other. Nothing else mattered.

— *Muriel Bach Diamond*

PREFACE

It was late summer of 1955 when I first arrived in Seattle, recently honorably discharged from the United States Navy. It seemed that Seattleites had two topics of conversation at the time—Boeing and Joe Diamond, not necessarily in that order. Some of the talk of Joe Diamond was less than complimentary. At my social level, he was seen as a greedy ogre anxious to separate the little people from their hard-earned money as they were forced to park in one of the many Diamond Parking lots.

I applied for work at Boeing as did almost every recent Seattle arrivee. They were on a hiring binge and were signing on anyone who could walk, crawl, or slither into their hiring center. I was turned down because it seems they didn't need any bombs or rockets loaded on their airplanes. It was the greatest good fortune for me, though I couldn't see it at the time. After a short stint with McHales service stations, I managed to secure employment with Windsor Garage and U-Drive, which was later to become Seattle U-Drive (subsequently to be purchased by Joe Diamond and John Cain), as the old, 1901 wooden parking garage was torn down to make room for a new, modern parking facility and the little company was forced to move to a new home at 812 Pike Street.

A short six years later, when I was 27, I was fated to meet the 6' 2" Joe Diamond. A "journeyman" car washer, I still worked for the same company owned by Dave Litvin with two other employees, Burnett Sams (known as Sammy) and a part-timer, Henry (Hank) Ader. Sammy and Hank were both in their midfifties at the time.

Litvin was somewhere around 65 years of age and complained frequently of what he had concluded was a weak heart (he lived well into his 90s) and, in fact, later had to have a pace-maker installed. He had amassed a respectable nest egg from many years of hard work in the parking garage and U-Drive business. The U-Drive companies were vastly different from the car rental entities with which we are familiar in these more modern times. Our cars more often than not were two or three (or more) years old and had been repaired many times to keep them serviceable. Dave fervently wished to retire and enjoy his autumn years with his wife, Jenny.

In 1961, in the market for additional parking locations, Joe Diamond approached his friend Litvin, whose property on 8th and Pike, with several small storefronts, was of interest for a future parking lot. Dave agreed that he would sell the property but only if he could sell the U-Drive company too. Having no knowledge of or interest in the car rental business,

Joe declined to buy the U-Drive company. Dave insisted that he either buy the entire package including Seattle U-Drive or he wouldn't consider any portion of the sale. That was the end of the discussion until a short time later when Litvin informed Joe that he knew someone who would like to buy and run the car rental company but didn't have enough money to make the deal. John Cain (known affectionately as Johnny), a local entrepreneur and someone whom Joe knew somewhat through the Parking Association, operated a highly successful Shell service station and parking lot on the corner of 9th and Olive and was interested in expanding his horizons to include a car rental business. The price for the small local car rental company, including its inventory of 28 mostly used cars was $50,000. Joe put up the $50,000 and took John Cain's promissory note for $25,000 to be repaid out of profits of the car rental business. Joe was now half owner of a business of which he knew nothing but which would soon would become an important part of his life.

Joe and Johnny agreed to keep Hank, Sammy, and me in their employ, and thus began my several decades of association with Joe Diamond.

In reading his story, you will undoubtedly find, as I did in my time with him, that Joe is a very special man. He is a master negotiator. He never swears and, in the years I have known him, never smoked (although he says he smoked cigars in his earlier years) and is, without question, the gentlest and least greedy man I've known. Further, he is absolutely honest and to his friends, associates, partners in his many endeavors, and employees, loyal to a fault.

This story is not about me or Seattle U-Drive or our long tenure as a Budget Rent a Car licensee for the states of Washington and Oregon, except as is necessary to the telling of Joe's story; nor is it for that matter about the highly successful, multistate Diamond Parking operations. It is about Joe Diamond the man.

Though Josef was born in California, his story begins in Russia.

CHAPTER ONE
THE IMMIGRATION
TO AMERICA

There was nothing easy about living in Russia as a Jew at the turn of the last century. Hikel Dimeretz (later to be known as Michael Diamond), Josef's father, worked hard and long as a village tailor in a small town near Kiev to provide for his family. He tried to keep his wife, Rifke, and their three small children, Louis, Jenny, and Sadie, as insulated as possible from the hatred toward Jews that was so prevalent in the village. The Jewish families were afraid to go out at night unless absolutely necessary and, when it couldn't be avoided, traveled with one or more companions for some small degree of safety. Animosity and violence toward them was everywhere. The lack of concern for the rights and welfare of Jews by government officials led to beatings and killings becoming commonplace. Assault or murder of a Jew at that time in Russia was not considered a criminal offense.

As was very accurately portrayed in the movie *Fiddler on the Roof*, the pressure was on Jews to leave the village … to leave Russia … to get out. Whether or not they had a place to go or the means to get there wasn't a matter of consideration. The non-Jewish Russians had been stirred up by government propaganda to demand their departure.

It was in this atmosphere of hatred and persecution of Russian Jews, and with the knowledge that he would almost certainly be drafted into the Russian army, leaving his family without any realistic means of support and forced to be a part of the very government that was promoting the bigotry against Jews, that Hikel made the decision to leave Russia and emigrate to New York, America, where he hoped to start a new life. His plan was to establish himself there and make sufficient money to send for Rifke and the three children. Knowing that their quality of life would continue to deteriorate as long as they remained in Russia, Rifke reluctantly agreed to suffer the anticipated long separation, hiding with the children in the basement of a loyal friend, with the hope that soon the entire family would be in the New World with a new and promising life ahead.

Leaving his homeland and the village that had been home for so many years for the unknown was enough of a traumatic experience. Leaving all of his loved ones behind made it nearly unbearable for Hikel, but he knew that there was no other answer to their plight, so he set his jaw and started on his journey.

When Hikel arrived in New York, he spoke no English. He had received no schooling in Russia and was as nearly unprepared to make a decent life in his adopted country as anyone had ever been. Hikel had one advantage, however. He was an experienced tailor who wasn't afraid to work as many hours a day as needed to succeed in this new land.

There is some question of how Hikel Dimeretz became Michael Diamond. One school of thought says that authorities at Ellis Island, finding some of the names of immigrants too difficult either to pronounce or to spell, arbitrarily chose names that were easier to handle on their records. Another account believes that Hikel chose the name because it sounded more American. Whichever the case, Hikel Dimeretz was now an American (though he still couldn't speak the language) named Michael Diamond.

Soon after his arrival in America, Michael traveled to Boston, where he as able to find employment with a clothing manufacturer. There he worked diligently and, while already a talented tailor, learned much about the mass manufacture of clothing. He sent letters to his wife and children regularly, but included no money and no invitation to join him in Boston. Though he lived frugally, he was unable to save enough money for their passage to join him in this country. It is possible too that Michael just *might* have been enjoying his "single" life a little too much. Whether or not that was the case will never be known for sure.

After three long years of waiting and dreaming of the reunion that evaded her, Mama Dimeretz lost patience. With her meager savings and the money she had managed to borrow, which was barely enough, she arranged passage on a tramp steamer heading for America. She boarded with her three children in tow and a few possessions tightly packed in nondescript boxes and bags. The nightmarish trip across the angry Atlantic, without any food to speak of and being consigned with hundreds of others to the rusty vessel's hold with no toilet facilities, would have been unbearable for anyone else, but Rifke was determined to find her husband. So, the little family endured the difficult journey with all the courage they could muster and a dream of better things to come. Many long days and nights of cold, moist air; hunger; the stench of human waste; and seasickness passed before the ship finally docked safely in New York.

The nightmare was only beginning. When she arrived at Ellis Island, Rifke found to her profound dismay that in all of New York and Boston her husband was nowhere to be found. While Hikel (which she always called him) had written to tell her that he had moved to Los Angeles, the letter had not arrived before her departure from Russia. The feeling of being abandoned must have been devastating. Being in a strange land and not able to speak the language and with three youngsters to take care of had to be a terrifying experience. With no friends or relatives to assist her in getting settled, the authorities decided Rifke must return to Russia. They can be forgiven for their failed attempt to dictate to this determined woman since they had no idea whom they had taken on as an adversary. As Josef said years later, "You didn't send my mother anywhere!"

Still in this country a full month later against the plaintive insistence of immigration authorities, and still without any knowledge of English, Rifke's search came to an end when she finally learned, with help from the immigration people who were most likely anxious to rid themselves of this strong-willed woman, that her prodigal husband was living and working in Los Angeles, California. Having just traveled the Atlantic Ocean without any money, it now became necessary for her and her children to cross the American continent, still without any money. Undaunted, Rifke set about contacting various charities until she put together enough money for train fare and a small basket of food. Along the way, she and the children were offered oranges and bananas by passengers whom they met as they traveled for three days and three nights to the West Coast. Having never seen such fruit, the children tried to eat them without bothering to remove the peels. Helpful fellow travelers offered suggestions on how to best consume the strange delicacies.

The train pulled into the station in Los Angeles, carrying an exhausted and not very happy Rifke and her children. They were finally reunited with Papa Diamond after the long and difficult separation. As Joe said many years later, "Mother must not have been too angry with Dad because I was born the very next year."

So began life for Joe Diamond, the first of the family to be born in the United States.

MEMORIES

During Joe Diamond's lifelong career as a lawyer and entrepreneur, in addition to his long list of friends, he has enjoyed the company of many loyal and devoted employees. Judy Ann Moulton, an accomplished actress, singer, and his executive assistant for over 15 years was no exception. In 1990, on the occasion of his 83rd birthday, she contacted many of the friends he had come to know over his many decades to help her create a "Book of Memories." Within the leather-bound book over four inches thick are the fond recollections of over 200 of his closest friends, clients, and associates.

Thanks to the hours of efforts by Judy Ann, these pages are filled with the comments of those who know and love Joe. Her own entry in the Book of Memories is worth mentioning here. "In 1988, when I interviewed to be Josef's secretary, he said, 'Well, I suppose I should tell you who I am.' I interrupted him to say that since my car had been barreled [attached by cable to a barrel for nonpayment of the parking fee on a Diamond Parking lot], I knew very well who he was. He laughed and said he was sorry. But I told him that it had been my fault and there was no need to be sorry. He eventually offered me the job and I accepted."

Speaking of the Book of Memories compiled by Judy Ann Moulton and referred to throughout this authorized biography, Muriel Bach Diamond, Joe Diamond's wife, wrote: "The day after I returned home from Chicago after an extended visit to greet my new grandson, I dis-

covered that Judy Ann Moulton, Joe's right hand at Short Cressman and Burgess, had contacted most of Joe's friends, relatives, business associates – even remote acquaintances—in order to put together this Book of Memories for his eighty-third birthday. But before taking this gigantic leap, lest the plan be unseemly, she first contacted Jerry Alhadeff for his approval. He encouraged her to go ahead full steam.

"When I learned the scope of this endeavor, I was astounded, for Judy not only works full time as a legal secretary to Joe, she is an actress and singer of note (no pun intended), often performing at such theaters as the Fifth Avenue. She also is married to David, for whom she surely must find some time to make him happy, too!

"Much as this book is a tribute to Joe, it must also be a tribute to Judy Ann Moulton, who knows that giving of oneself is the key to happiness. She has my profound gratitude for undertaking a task of such enormity for the man I treasure."

Upon being presented with the leather-covered Book of Memories, Joe Diamond wrote this letter to all who contributed:

Dear Friend,

Sorry I can't be more personal but with over 200 responses (am I flattered)—Your comments in a page in my Book of Memories is indeed appreciated—forever.

It was a complete surprise to me and I thought I knew what went on in my office. How Judy (my secretary) could have *accomplished it all without my even being suspicious is hard to understand. But she is accomplished.*

Anyway, as a total surprise to me, I walked into the coffee room at 3 p.m. on my birthday and it was jammed with well-wishers—or maybe they only wanted some excellent birthday cake.

I was presented a beautiful "Book of Memories" filled with a page or two from each of you (over 200—not pages—people) and Judy threw out all the uncomplimentary remarks—so it did all go to my head. Thanks.

It's hard to understand that you would all take time to write and say such nice things about an old lawyer and someone who locks barrels on your cars.

It was a wonderful birthday and well worth waiting 83 years to celebrate—because of what you did. And even if you didn't mean all of the nice things you said, I'm going to believe you did for all of the next 83 years. I'm only halfway there.

Thanks for the memories,
Joe Diamond

CHAPTER TWO
SEATTLE'S ALASKA-YUKON FAIR BECKONS

Little Josef was but two years old when his father became intrigued by the effect the Alaska gold rush was having on the Seattle area, with the Alaska-Yukon Exposition bringing rapid growth and related business potential. Though the family was getting by in Los Angeles, Papa Michael decided that they should pack up their belongings once again and move to Seattle, where he envisioned he would have a much better opportunity to become a success.

The family, now seven in number as younger brother Leon had also been born in California, journeyed to Seattle without any guarantee of employment but with the continuing dream of prospering in America. In those first few months, young Josef and his siblings slept on doors, positioned on sawhorses, that Papa Diamond had removed from their hinges so the children could sleep above the floor. It wasn't easy at first, but Michael soon became very busy in the garment industry and started building what would prove to be a successful clothing business in which he was the designer, cutter, and master tailor. His continuing success was the more impressive considering that, as Joe Diamond has said, "Neither of my parents ever spent a day in school. My father could sign his name, but that was all."

As Michael anticipated, Seattle was booming. It was 1909 and the Alaska gold rush was in full swing. As the major jumping off port for those eager fortune hunters going to and from Alaska, Seattle's growth was phenomenal. It was in this exciting atmosphere that Michael began to develop his dream. His eagerness to provide for his family and his willingness to put in long hours of hard work was the secret as his business grew. He began to employ people just to keep up with the demand for his clothing. Josef's sister Rose was born during these times; life was finally good for Michael and Rifke (now known as Ruby) Diamond.

Josef was a good, if independent, student in elementary school and because of his good grades was allowed to skip the eighth grade and go on to high school directly. Though his first high school was called East High School, it didn't last long. The young teenager worked one summer to help tear down the temporary structures that had constituted East High in order to make room for a new building.

Construction of the new school proceeded quickly as there were no interminable delays caused by environmental studies

Michael and Ruby Diamond and family

and impact statements in the early 1900s. Soon Garfield High, whose name had been chosen by young Joe and the other first students, was, as Joe tells us, "open for business and learning with the aid of a hickory stick."

Joe acquitted himself well in high school and was part of the first graduating class of Garfield High in 1924. That first class included many of Joe's boyhood friends, who would eventually become civic leaders. These included luminaries such as Charles O. Carroll, who would later become King County prosecutor; Ed Munro, who was destined to be a King County commissioner; Melvin J. R. Williams, who would one day find himself county treasurer; eventual city comptroller Carl Erlandson; and John M. Nelson, who would head up Seattle City Light.

Upon graduation, like most young men in that day and age, Joe set out to find a job. In her matriarchal role, his mother informed him that he was not going to go to work but instead would enroll at the University of Washington. Puzzled, Joe asked, "Why would you want me to go college when my older brother and sisters haven't?" She informed him then, on no uncertain terms, that he was going to be a doctor or a lawyer. "But I can't be a doctor—the sight of blood makes me faint," Joe confided. "So, you'll be a lawyer," commanded Mother Diamond.

In accordance with mama's wishes, Joe dutifully applied, and was accepted at the University of Washington at 17 years of age due to his having been allowed to skip one year of elementary school. He found college life to his liking. In addition to making many new friends, he was enjoying the learning challenges it presented when, after only one semester, he found it necessary to drop out for a time. He relates, "My father had moved his business to Canada and left me behind to close out the old business, which included the selling of all of the material, equipment, furniture, and fixtures. I was 17 years old at the time." Once that daunting task was completed, Joe joined his family in Vancouver, British Columbia, 150 miles north of Seattle just across the border, where he became involved with his father in his business there. That business was growing briskly thanks to the hard work and the innate knowledge of the garment market of Papa Diamond. Joe was put in charge of adorning cloth coats and jackets with fur collars and cuffs, which were very much in vogue at the time.

MEMORIES

"I met Joe in 1918 and we became friends," wrote Bernard Ordell. "As kids, we organized a roller skate hockey team. Another time, we hitch-hiked to Tacoma to go to the automobile races. In the summertime we used to meet at the playing field and play a game called buck-buck before spectators. Joe was just one of the boys, and we remained friends through the years."

"Joe was once described to me as a bear in sheep's clothing, but in reality, Joe is a sheep in bear's clothing. The man I have come to know is loyal and sensitive and expects the same from those around him. He also expects competence, understanding, and measured responses. His story is larger than life. I am better off having known Joe."

– William P. Anderson, a friend

"Joe became a good friend and more than an attorney over the years, counseling me in both good and troubled times. As much as I have tried to remain cool and calm, by nature I am a worrier. Joe noticed this trait in me and always told me, 'Wait to worry.' Those three words changed my outlook on life and made me a more stable and healthy person. It is such a practical and logical theory and it per-sonifies Joe's character—practical and logical. It is remarkable how many troubling conditions work themselves out. When I look back, there was no need to worry. Many times I said to myself, 'Thanks, Joe, for those three words—you saved me needless hours of anxiety and pressure!'"

– Sam LeBid

"You have been a wonderful counselor, advisor, and friend both to me and many others in our community. Thank you for your service to your fellow man."

– John Miller
United States Congressman

"About 1919 [70 years ago] we were 12-year-olds on a summer vacation, and it apparently was a pleasant experience for me because he still reminds me of our long-gone summertime adventure."

– Bill Rosen

Josef Diamond, center 2nd row

CHAPTER THREE
DIAMOND PARKING IS BORN

A year went by before, due to his mother's insistence, Joe finally returned to the University of Washington where he offset his attendance costs by working for his older brother, mechanically gifted Louis, who had started an auto service and repair company with a small parking area in downtown Seattle. Louis had acquired the business upon graduating from high school. It was located on 4th Avenue and Pike Street across from where Bon-Macy's is currently, but not much was there at the time. He had built a drive-up rack (possibly the first one anywhere) so that he could get under an automobile to service it. There were very few cars in the area in those early days. There was the usual assortment of Model Ts, Hupmobiles, the occasional Stanley Steamer, a few Cadillacs, and something developed by Louis Chevrolet. Most of these machines belonged to—who else?—doctors and dentists who worked in the Medical-Dental Building nearby. As these cars were often left for the entire day (that is the ones that had not been picked up and delivered, which was another part of Louis's service) after having been serviced, the lot became so crowded as to limit his ability to take on drive-up customers, so Louis began to charge a dime a day for parking. That thinned out the number of cars left for the day and provided space for others who might need repairs, service, or temporary parking. It wasn't long before Louis discovered that he could make more money parking cars than he was making for servicing and repairing them. "That's where it all started," relates Joe, "in the year 1922."

As a sophomore in high school Joe earned money to help finance his education by working at his brother's business. "We hand-pumped gas from a 500-gallon tank that we had mounted on wheels in order to move from car to car," reports Joe with a note of pride in his voice over Louis's ingenuity in creating the portable fueling arrangement. Additionally, Joe kept very busy parking customers' cars after school and during summer break. Even during college and law school he continued to work with Louis for extra income and to assist in the growing business while his brother added locations to his small parking company. Before Joe went on active duty with the army in 1940, Louis had built his parking company up to 17 locations in Seattle.

Joe majored in business administration in a combined course that included several prelaw courses at the University of Washington and graduated with a BA in 1928. Even though his personal dream was to be an architect, and later in life he did design many buildings, including his lovely home on Lake Washington (at least he had a heavy influence on what the architect produced), Josef's mother made it quite clear that his choices did not include that field. Accordingly, he enrolled in law school. While in his first year at the University of Washington Law School, the stock market crash of October 1929 had its devastating effect on everyone's plans, including Josef's. With previously wealthy people jumping out of windows of tall buildings in New York and millions out of work and standing in line at soup kitchens, the future didn't look very promising to a young man looking forward to graduating with a law degree, passing the bar, and going into practice.

It was in his last year of law school that Joe began to consider other options for when he completed his studies. He was concerned that, due to the depression, the opportunities for employment as a lawyer would be minimal. "Without discussing it with my mother," Joe admits, "I took the big step and signed up for a U.S. Navy flying cadet course, satisfied that I would become a navy pilot. I planned to complete the eight months of required evening extension courses for the navy at about the same time I received my law degree."

Following that, once commissioned as an ensign, Joe expected to honor his obligation to the navy by reporting to Sand Point Navy Base in Seattle, whence he would be sent to the flight training facility in Pensacola, Florida. Four years of active duty flying biplanes from the flight deck of such early aircraft carriers as the USS *Langley* or the USS *Saratoga* were expected to follow. The salary for navy pilots at the time was $400 a month, an extremely handsome rate of pay in 1930.

Alas, upon earning his law degree, receiving his commission in the navy, and, shortly afterward, passing the bar in June 1931, Joe finally told his mother of his responsibility to the navy. She would have no part of that kind of an arrangement. According to Joe, she had a "fit." She said, "I didn't raise my son to become a soldier." She informed him that he would *not* go into the military and *would* seek employment as a lawyer. An obedient son, Joe agreed but hedged that if he was not successful in finding a position with a law office by the end of summer, he would report to the navy at Sand Point in August. His mother made him promise that he would immediately begin looking for a job as a lawyer. He set about trying to find employment with a law firm.

MEMORIES

"I got acquainted with Joe in the late 1930s when I was deputy prosecuting attorney in King County and later, when I had my own law practice with Lloyd Shorett in the Smith Tower in Seattle. When I was chairman of the Washington State Crime Commission in the state senate, investigating organized crime throughout the state of Washington, Joe was representing some interests in Gray's Harbor that didn't want the committee hearing held in that area. As chairman, I had scheduled the hearings and had subpoenaed the police chief, the assistant police chief, the head of the vice squad, and many of the madams who were running houses of prostitution in the area. Lo and behold, before we had a chance to hold the meeting, Joe succeeded in getting a temporary injunction to stop us. This held up our proceedings several months because the matter was argued first in the Thurston County Superior

Court and then it actually went to the Washington State Supreme Court. Finally, the supreme court allowed us to move ahead and hold our hearings. We re-scheduled them and, of course, Joe appeared on behalf of different witnesses whom we called in, primarily members of the Aberdeen Police Department. The hearings lasted about a week so we had a good opportunity to litigate against each other, in a sense, even though ours was an investigating committee. But, after that, we always remained friends."

– Albert D. Rosellini
Former governor of Washington

Dr. John D. Hicks wrote: "When you spend some time talking to Joe you realize what an extraordinary life he has led. I have been after him to write an autobiography. His experiences in the army during WWII, his pioneering business adventures into discount stores such as Gov-Mart, and his many other business experiences while, at the same time, running a highly successful law practice would make a fascinating story. Not only would it tell the story of a remarkable person but also cover an important period in the history of our country."

CHAPTER FOUR
HANG YOUR HAT
IN THE LIBRARY

With a list he had laboriously prepared of every law firm in the phone book arranged alphabetically by building and then by floor, Joe began calling on each of the city's law firms (even in those early days there were several hundred of them). Unlike many modern-day employment seekers who mail out résumés, Joe, clad in a newly acquired suit, began wearing out shoe leather in those warm July days. He took the elevator to the top floor of each building in Seattle and worked his way down the stairs to street level. Building by building, floor by floor, firm by firm, over a period of several days he heard the same disappointing "Sorry, no openings."

Disheartened but determined, Joe went over his list again. He had been particularly impressed with the firm of Caldwell and Lycette. Not only was it one of the most highly respected law firms in Seattle, but Hugh Caldwell was a civic leader, having been Seattle's mayor. Joe called a second time on Caldwell and

Lycette in the Exchange Building. With some ingenuity, he worked his way past the receptionist and, with no small amount of trepidation, the 24-year-old, recently graduated lawyer began to make his case with senior partner, Mr. Caldwell.

"Hugh Caldwell was sitting at his desk. I reminded him that I had been in to see him a short time ago and that he had told me he was not hiring. I told him that I realized I did not know how to practice law, but I needed experience and didn't want any pay while gaining it. I told him I wanted to continue my legal education in the real world and learn about the practice of law. I asked if I could be helpful in running errands, doing research and briefings. I told him that I wanted to learn more about the practice of law." Caldwell, taken aback, informed our hungry-to-learn young man that he not only didn't need him but, whether or not he was working for nothing, they had no office that he could use. Joe responded that he'd be willing to work in the library. "If you'll allow me to sit in the library, I could learn a great deal in 30 days and then I'll leave." Running out of objections and arguments as to why he couldn't use this pro bono assistance, Caldwell said, "Young man, if you want to hang your hat in the library for 30 days, help yourself!"

A week or so later, with a liberal dose of embarrassment, Joe went to see the commanding officer at Sand Point Naval Air Station to inform him that he would not be reporting to the navy in August as he had secured a job as lawyer. He neglected to mention that he was not going to be paid and that the job was of only a 30-day duration. The navy captain's jaw dropped, and with the veins in his neck pulsating, he told our seemingly naïve young lawyer, "You can't just quit the navy! You will report here as ordered on August first. In the meantime you will go to Bremerton Naval Shipyard and draw your uniform!"

Apologetically, Joe informed the C.O. that he had promised his mother that he would get a job as a lawyer and that she would not allow him to report to the navy. Infuriated and becoming red in the face, the officer shouted, "You promised who?" Now with his face turning even a brighter shade of red and not allowing an opportunity for a response, he hollered, "Young man, you get off this base, and don't you ever come back!" Joe was out of the navy. Whew! That was a relief. Not the "getting out of the navy" part but the "now able to face his mother" part.

Single at the time, Joe worked for Caldwell and Lycette running errands, doing research and briefings from first thing in the morning until late in the evening. In his own natural way of empathizing with others in trouble, he sent polite letters out to clients who hadn't paid their bills and whom the law firm hadn't pressed very hard for payment because times were so tough. His letters, on law office stationery, resulted in numbers of past due accounts, from clients with little money for anything but survival, being paid up. Without drawing a cent of pay, Joe was making good use of his time and bringing in money for the firm in addition to a number of other necessary functions.

All too soon his 30 days were over, so Joe presented himself in Mr. Caldwell's office to say good-bye. "He asked where I was going. I said I didn't know where, but my time was up and I was leaving as agreed. Mr. Caldwell asked, 'How much are we paying you?' and I reminded him that I was working without pay. He said, 'You go back to work; you are getting $100 a month.'" A hundred dollars a month? In 1931 it was not only a handsome salary but many of Joe's law school classmates who had managed to find a job in the legal field because of a connection, such as a family member being a partner, were being paid $25 a month and pleased to get it. "I became a partner in that firm four years later, and they changed the name on the door to Caldwell, Lycette and Diamond," Joe relates with a certain deserved pride in his voice.

Now an official member of the firm, Joe took on his first case, involving a man who had been in an automobile accident driving along a narrow, dusty old country road south of Renton, Washington.

A truck had approached from the opposite direction, occupying more of the road than it was entitled to. With a collision imminent, Joe's client veered off the road on the right-hand side and bounced down into a deep ditch, where his vehicle crashed into a thicket of blackberry brambles before it came to rest. While the driver wasn't seriously injured, his automobile was in dire shape. Even the dents had dents.

C2 Seattle Post-Intelligencer, Tuesday, October 7, 1986

Work for free to prove yourself

ANN LANDERS

Dear Ann Landers: The job seeker today needs someone to talk to him (or her) like a "Dutch uncle" (or aunt).

Even though a lot of folks in this country think we are enjoying an era of great prosperity there are still millions of people out of work. Here is some advice for job applicants (especially young people).

The first thing that pops out of their mouth is, "How much vacation time do I get?" "What is your medical plan and is there a retirement guarantee?"

If you are really smart you won't ask those questions. You will offer to work free for a week to prove your worth. Such an applicant is irresistible. — Employed in Calif.

Dear Cal: Terrific advice. One of the most successful lawyers in Seattle did just that. He applied for a job in a law firm during the Depression, offering to work for nothing for a month. During the month he was the first in the office and the last to leave. He worked Saturdays and Sundays. After a month they wouldn't *let* him leave. Today Joe Diamond is the top man in that firm.

Joe made his appearance for his client in district court, where he soon discovered that the presiding judge was also the local barber. He chuckled to himself, thinking, "This is interesting. My first case in court is going to be presented to and decided by a small-town barber."

Joe won a judgment of $400 for his client. His confidence increased as did the confidence of the senior partners in the firm. Soon other cases would be assigned to him.

Not long after winning the case before the barber cum judge, Joe's second case was to represent his friend Sol Rubin, who was a fur trader. Rubin had been charged with buying beaver furs out of season. He was brought to trial in King County District Court on criminal charges.

"During the trial," Joe later recalled, "the trapper who had allegedly sold the furs to Rubin testified that he had caught the beavers near where he lived in Olympia, Washington." Joe continued, "He said he brought them into town and sold them to my friend Sol, whom I was now representing. The trapper admitted trapping the beavers out of season. He also testified that my friend Sol was the one who bought the pelts."

These events, even if true, wouldn't have been a serious matter, but for Joe's client they were. "You see," Joe said, "my friend and client had lived in Seattle for 20 years. He had two young daughters who were born here, but he was not a U.S. citizen. He was a Canadian. So a conviction in this case would mean that Sol would be deported back to Canada after having lived and raised a family in Seattle for all those years."

Sol convinced Joe that he hadn't bought the beaver furs; the trapper who had testified that he sold them to Sol was lying. Further, the trapper was a friend of Sol's, and Sol couldn't understand why a friend would do this to him. Though he had bought many furs from his trapper friend in the past, he insisted that he never bought furs off season.

In court, Sol Rubin's "friend" described the sale of the furs in minute detail which convinced the jury that he was telling the truth. Sol was convicted.

"I believed my client," Joe said, "so I decided there had to be another explanation for all of this. I couldn't allow this conviction to stand, so I talked to the prosecuting attorney, who I knew and said, 'Pete, I'm going to try to prove to you that the trapper was lying and, if I do, will you dismiss the case?' Pete chuckled and said, 'Of course—the trapper's testimony is the only evidence we have. If you can prove it's untrue, I'll dismiss it.'"

The following night, Joe made the 30-mile drive to Olympia and, with not very clear directions from Sol, spent much of the night searching in the wind and rain before locating the trapper's fairly well-maintained cabin in a remote area. Joe was invited in.

"I told him that I knew he was a good friend of Sol's and that I was surprised by his testimony," Joe explained. "Reminding him how Sol had once bought gifts for his children, I finally said, 'Since Sol tells me he did not buy those furs off season, I'm wondering why you would testify against him in that way?'

"'Well,' the grizzled trapper replied while slowly stroking his thick mustache, 'I'll tell you. I did sell those furs out of season, but not to Sol. I sold 'em to a fur broker across the road. Sol's such an important guy around Seattle, I thought he would get out of this thing without any trouble. I figured it'd be more difficult for the other buyer. So, that's why I laid it all on Sol.'"

The next day, satisfied that he had been able to vindicate his friend with the overnight visit, Joe relayed the story to the prosecuting attorney. After he was able to verify Joe's story, he dropped the charges as promised. Even though there had been a conviction, Joe managed to get the case dismissed.

There was a matter involving Joe collecting an overdue bill that should be of interest here. He sent a letter to a man (I won't use his real name) who hadn't paid his account at the Stimson Building Garage.

CALDWELL & LYCETTE
2001-2005 EXCHANGE BUIILDING
SEATTLE
ELIOT 1331
November 21, 1933

Mr. John Public
1234 Main Street
Seattle, Washington
Re: <u>Stimson Building Garage. Account</u>

Dear Sir:

The Stimson Building Garage has turned over to us for the purpose of filing suit against you, your unpaid and past due indebtedness to them in the sum of $2.00.

A lawsuit on this matter will of course add a great deal of additional expense to you in the way of court costs, sheriff's fees, and attorneys' fees. We trust that it will not be necessary to take legal action, and we shall endeavor to save you the additional cost thereof, provided you cooperate with us in this entire matter.

Please get in touch with us immediately and make payment of this small account, if you desire to avoid court litigation.

Very truly yours,
CALDWELL & LYCETTE
By and signed Josef Diamond

That must have been in the days when two bucks were still two bucks!

MEMORIES

Ann Landers, known to many of us as Eppie Lederer, wife of the co-founder of Budget Rent A Car, Jules Lederer, included this in her column in the Seattle Post-Intelligencer *on October 7, 1986:*

Dear Ann Landers:

The job seeker today needs someone to talk to him (or her) like a "Dutch uncle" (or aunt). Even though a lot of folks in this country think we are enjoying an era of great prosperity there are still millions of people out of work. Here is some advice for job applicants (especially young people). The first thing that pops out of their mouth is, "How much vacation time do I get?" "What is your medical plan and is there a retirement guarantee?" If you are really smart you won't ask those questions. You will offer to work free for a week to prove your worth. Such an applicant is irresistible.

— Employed in Calif.

Dear Cal.:

Terrific advice. One of the most successful lawyers in Seattle did just that. He applied for a job in a law firm during the Depression, offering to work for nothing for a month. During the month, he was the first in the office and the last to leave. He worked Saturdays and Sundays. After a month they wouldn't let him leave. Today Joe Diamond is the top man in that firm.

"Sometimes when my husband Dorwin and I would have a lively 'discussion' because of opposing views. Dorwin would laugh and recall his long-ago days in college when he, as a budding law student, would have friendly 'debates' with his fellow law students. Perhaps they were practicing for the courtroom. And I especially remember my husband describing, with gusto, that in those long-forgotten 'word duels,' Josef Diamond was extremely adept and skillful in asserting his views. Dorwin used to say

that Josef would sometimes announce, in jest, that in spite of my husband being a native of Wichita, Kansas, he was 'pretty smart for a country boy.' Dorwin would always laugh at that fond memory. But the most memorable thing about Josef is that, in spite of his remarkable accomplishments and achievements and importance and fame, he is utterly unaffected and natural, and he took pains to put me at ease and to see that I was comfortable and enjoying myself as his dinner guest. Unforgettable."

– Ronaye Cook

"My respect for Josef Diamond has grown through the years into admiration. He is demanding but fair, clinically objective but compassionate, and immensely loyal to his family and friends. He is NOT one of those to whom Oliver Wendell Holmes referred when he said, 'Lawyers spend a great deal of time shoveling smoke.'"

– John D. Mangles
Chairman, Security Pacific Bank

"When I first entered Josef's office as a young rabbi in my midtwenties, he received me with dignity and respect, and he gave of his time, notwithstanding his very, very busy schedule. Joe Diamond represents the true work ethic that has made our country great. He is a true patriot. He is a strong family man in a society where that particular trait is not as fashionable as it once was. His mother used to call him 'Yossele,' and he is deserving of the old saying from the Talmud 'May you go from strength to strength.'"

– Rabbi S. B. Levitin

"Joe Diamond was a gentleman when I met him in 1932 and has always been a gentleman."

– Ralph Schoenfeld

CHAPTER FIVE
THE WILL

There came a day in 1933 when Hugh Caldwell stepped into Joe's office with a look of deep concern. Joe waited for him to speak. "Joe, I had an inquiry from a friend of mine, a woman who lives in California, who is concerned about her aunt who is dying." Joe listened intently as he continued. "Her aunt, Mrs. Clark, is wealthy and living in a nursing home here in Seattle. My friend has heard rumors from a nurse at the facility that her aunt has made a will in which she has left everything to her banker and her lawyer and cut the family off completely. Would you look into the matter and see what can be done?" Joe quickly agreed to take on the task.

He didn't much like the antiseptic smell of the nursing home (he said it always reminded him of death and bedpans) as he sat across from Mrs. Clark in her room. Frail and 98 years old, she swayed back and forth as she stroked a hot water bottle with her thin, spotted arm.

"Mrs. Clark, my name is Joe Diamond. Can we talk for a few minutes?"

"This is my baby," she said as she continued to stroke her hot water bottle. "Oh … uh … yes. Mrs. Clark, I would like to talk to you about your will." "This is my baby." "Mrs. Clark, did you recently make up a will?" "This is my baby." Joe correctly concluded that he wasn't going to get anything further from her.

"That's all you're gonna get." The voice was that of a large nurse who had entered the room and was standing behind Joe in her stiffly starched white uniform. "Did I hear you mention something about her will?" "Yes, I did," responded Joe. The nurse continued, "A couple weeks ago a lawyer and a man who said he was her banker were here to visit Mrs. Clark. They had a will with them that they asked her to sign." Pleased to hear that someone had some knowledge of what had happened, Joe asked, "Did she sign?" "Oh yeah, she signed it. Me and Nurse Crane were both witnesses. They left a copy for Mrs. Clark here in her night stand." The nurse opened the drawer and produced the will for Joe to read.

As far as Joe had determined through his checking when he was asked to take the case, the woman in California was perhaps Mrs. Clark's only living relative, but the document provided for her entire estate to be left to the lawyer and the banker in equal shares. He knew the two men who would be the beneficiaries of the will. They were well known and well respected, but everything about the matter smelled of skull-duggery. "Yes," Joe thought, "one could say with a degree of certainty that foul play was afoot … and an arm … and a leg." "I'll get back to you," Joe told the nurse as he left.

On his way back to his office, in what was then considered to be heavy traffic, he considered the situation. There were more than a few ways he could approach this problem, he thought. His thought process continued, "I could wait until Mrs. Clark dies and then contest the probate of the will as being signed by someone who was incompetent at the time of signing, but that would put me at odds with two very prominent and reputable men, a banker and a lawyer, who will almost certainly be testifying that she was indeed competent when she signed the document." The matter was further complicated by the fact that the lawyer involved had been one of Joe's professors at the University of Washington. Not that Joe would shrink from taking on the onerous task under those circumstances but, he reasoned, there might be a less complicated way to accomplish the same end.

Once in his office, he caused two wills to be drawn up for Mrs. Clark. One was a simple document that canceled all previous wills and established that she was intestate at her death. Simply, the document would establish that she died without a will, in which case her estate would go to any relatives, whoever they might be. The second will left Mrs. Clark's entire estate to her only apparent living relative, the niece in California.

Placing a phone call to the nurse with whom he had spoken earlier, Joe explained that he was sending her both wills and asked her to have Mrs. Clark sign either one of them if she should have a lucid moment.

Two weeks later, the cooperative nurse called to inform him, "I had Mrs. Clark sign the wills." "That's fine," responded Joe, "which one did she sign?" "Oh, I had her sign both of them." Somewhat stunned, he asked, "Both of them? Which one did she sign last?" The confused nurse responded, "I don't know … I don't know which one she signed last." Incredulous but pragmatic, Joe thought, "If that's the way it is, so be it." He thanked the nurse and asked that she inform him when Mrs. Clark passed away. He retrieved the wills and filed them in his office.

It was several months later when Joe heard from the nurse that Mrs. Clark had died. Knowing that time wasn't on his side, he took the will that canceled all previous wills leaving everything to her heirs, whoever they might be, and had it filed for probate immediately, before the banker and lawyer could put their highly questionable will into effect. Then the waiting began.

Ten days went by before he heard from the involved lawyer. The measured voice on the other end asked, "Joe, I noticed in the *Daily Journal* that you filed a will for probate for Mrs. Clark?" "That's right, I did." "Do you think she was competent when she signed your will?" Somewhat amused, Joe answered, "I don't really know, but she was as competent as she has been for over a year—I know that."

That was the end of the strained but polite conversation and, once again, the waiting game began. It soon became apparent that the will Joe had prepared for Mrs. Clark was not going to be contested. The will was probated with the result that Joe had won nearly $800,000 (a massive fortune in the early 1930s) for the California niece, money that would not enhance the personal accounts of the lawyer and banker no doubt much to their dismay. They must have muttered to themselves the often uttered words of the TV cartoon character, Snidely Whiplash, "Curses … foiled again!"

And so it went from 1931 to 1935, when the name on the door of the law office was changed to Caldwell, Lycette and Diamond. Young Joe was a partner! The momentous occasion was announced in the *Seattle Times,* where Joe was described as "a modest, amiable 29-year-old attorney who, although just four years out of law school, this week became a partner in one of Seattle's leading law firms." A picture of a tall, handsome young man with a thin mustache making him appear like a stand-in for Douglas Fairbanks Jr. accompanied the story. As Joe tells the story, he still seems incredulous when he says, "The article in the *Times* was the first I knew that I had been made a partner."

The University of Washington

To all to whom these Letters shall come, Greeting:

The Regents of the University on recommendation of the University Faculty and by virtue
of the Authority vested in Them by Law have this day admitted

Josef Diamond

to the degree of

Juris Doctor

and have granted all the Rights, Privileges and Honors thereto pertaining
in recognition of completion June 15, 1931 of the requirements for this degree.

Given at Seattle in the State of Washington this fifth day of September in the year of our Lord
one thousand nine hundred and sixty-eight and of the University the one hundred and eighth.

President of the University

President of the Board of Regents

Dean

Josef Diamond Made Partner

— *1936*

A modest, amiable 29-year-old attorney who, although just five years out of law school, this week became a partner in one of Seattle's leading law firms — Josef Diamond, son of Mr. and Mrs. Michel Diamond—today was being congratulated by friends.

In recognition of his brilliant legal talents, the young attorney was made a partner with Hugh M. Caldwell, ex-mayor of Seattle and Deputy Imperial Potentate of the Shrine, and John P. Lycette,

Josef Diamond

veteran lawyer, in the new firm of Caldwell, Lycette & Diamond.

Born in Los Angeles, Mr. Diamond will celebrate his thirtieth birthday March 6. He was a member of Garfield High School's first graduating class in 1924, was graduated from the University of Washington Business Administration School in 1929 and won his law degree at the University in 1931, when his association with Caldwell & Lycette began.

The new law firm's offices are at 2001-6 Exchange Bldg.

HUGH M. CALDWELL AND JOHN P. LYCETTE

ANNOUNCE THE ASSOCIATION OF

JOSEF DIAMOND

WITH THEIR LAW OFFICES AT

2001 - 2006 EXCHANGE BUILDING
SECOND AVENUE AND MARION STREET

SEATTLE, WASHINGTON   TELEPHONE - ELIOT 1331

1931

CALDWELL & LYCETTE

ANNOUNCE THE ASSOCIATION OF

JOSEF DIAMOND

AS A PARTNER IN THE FIRM OF

CALDWELL, LYCETTE & DIAMOND

FOR THE GENERAL PRACTICE OF LAW

ELIOT 1331   LAW OFFICES:
SEATTLE, WASHINGTON   2001-5 EXCHANGE BLDG.

1934

MEMORIES

"I have been trying to remember when I first met Joe and, when thinking back, it seems like I have always known him. As long as I can recall he has always been our attorney and friend. My father told me of the time (I'm not sure of the year) he and my grandfather were involved in a lawsuit over some trivial situation. Joe represented the other side and, according to my dad, no one gave Joe a chance of winning. In fact, Joe and our attorney bet a new briefcase on the outcome. Needless to say, Joe won and from then on my father decided he wanted Joe to represent our side in any future legal matters. Over the years I have called on Joe many times for advice and he always seems to have the right answer.

– Patrick Druxman

"The time was early in May 1933. We occupied adjoining offices on the 20th floor of the Exchange Building. He was a young lawyer, and I was trying to get a start in the insurance business. Both of us must have joined the Junior Chamber of Commerce at about the same time and we served as board members for about three years. In 1950, when I decided to open an insurance agency under my own name and management, there was only one choice I could make when I needed a lawyer. Joe became one of our corporate directors. His counsel and advice were of great help. I believe that his greatest contributions were not business referrals but examples and lessons he taught me about integrity and honesty. I learned from him that a verbal agreement was just as binding as though it had been confirmed in writing. Also, he never was too busy to lend a helping hand when a personal problem arose. I could give many examples, but they would involve others and take much too long to write or read.

– Robinson Jenner

"I have no special stories about our long friendship [from 1934] other than to say he has always befriended me and I regard him as a scholarly, loving, handsome gentleman, and I wish him the very best for the remainder of his life."

– Mary Louise Reiter

CHAPTER SIX
JOE GOES INTO THE ARMY

Not many years after Joe made his lasting impression on the navy, Larry Carlson, another lawyer in the Caldwell and Lycette office, who was a friend, suggested that Joe should get a commission in the army reserve. He chuckled at the idea. What did he want with the army? But Carlson persisted and told Joe that it would be easy. All he had to do was to take a few night courses and he'd have his commission with no obligations, no meetings, and no active duty.

With his recent bride, Violett, pregnant at the time, he had no desire to commit himself to having to serve with the army, but his friend assured him that there was no risk and, with rumblings of possible war in Europe, it would be better to have a commission than to be called up to serve as an enlisted man. Joe reluctantly signed up, took the necessary courses, and eight months later, he received notice that he was now a captain in the United States Army Reserve. Carlson was right. Joe had his commission, and that was the end of it ... until 1941.

In the spring of 1941, Joe received a call from a captain in the army, who asked him if he would like to serve on active duty. What a question! Of course he didn't want active duty. He was busy with his burgeoning law practice, and he and Violett now had two children at home. He simply didn't have time for that nonsense. The captain said it was only a request, so Joe said no.

Only a month went by before another call came from the same captain. The army needed another lawyer to serve on active duty on the Judge Advocate General's staff at Fort Lewis between Tacoma and Olympia. Once again Joe declined the offer. The captain warned that it was within the realm of possibility that, one of these days, he might be calling and it wouldn't be a request.

A short time later, the captain again contacted Joe and said that he'd found a position where Joe might be willing to serve. General Thompson, of the Judge Advocate General's office at Camp Murray, next to Fort Lewis, needed a lawyer to handle legal problems involving draftees. Matters of conscientious objectors and other problems needed attention. The caller left Joe with the understanding that he might soon be ordered to report for active duty whether or not he agreed and might be sent to some overseas station. Joe said he would think it over. After discussing it with Vi (his pet name for Violett) during a short vacation at Harrison Hot Springs in Canada, Joe decided he would go to see General Thompson, and he did, the following week.

General Thompson informed Joe that he would be required to be on the post daily at 8:00 a.m. and that he would be free to return to Seattle at 4:00 p.m. Joe respectfully objected to those hours due to his need to attend to his law practice and take care of his family obligations. After much discussion with a lot of give and take, they arrived at a compromise so that Joe could show up somewhere around 11:00 a.m. and, if needed, depart the base at around 3:00 p.m. on any day. Further, it wouldn't be absolutely necessary to show up on Wednesdays since Wednesdays were set as a half day anyway. Joe's reasoning was that it wouldn't make sense for him to show up at 11:00 a.m. and leave at noon. The logic was inescapable, even for the army. The same logic applied easily to the other half day, Saturday. So, it became part of the understanding that Joe wouldn't have to show up on either Wednesday or Saturday. It was also agreed that if he got stuck in a trial or other legal matter that required his undivided attention in Seattle, he needn't show up at all so long as he called the base to inform them of the situation.

With the understanding to Joe's satisfaction, the matter of a uniform came up. Joe didn't have a uniform and was loath to have to change in and out of a uniform to take care of his army obligation as well as his law practice. The general finally agreed that, as an army lawyer he really didn't need to wear a uniform. So that was the understanding. "With that I had to make up my mind—yes or no to active duty." Joe tells us.

Joe agreed to go home and discuss the matter with Vi, but first, to make sure that everyone was on the same page, Joe offered, "Let's see if we understand each other ..." and went on to step through each of the details of the understanding they had reached. The general agreed that each portion of the agreement was clearly understood but added, "And those are the last concessions I'm going to make. Take it or leave it." Joe said that after he discussed the matter with Vi he would report to the general the next week as to his decision. He decided in favor of the army partially because of the flexibility he would have under General Thompson.

Then came the day when General Thompson was reassigned and a new judge advocate general took over. Joe's new "boss" was General DeLong. Wondering if the arrangement he had with General Thompson was in jeopardy of being a thing of the past, Joe thought about discussing his arrangement with the new general, but before he had a chance to do so, he was summoned to the general's office.

"I see you coming and going at odd hours, and I never see you in uniform. You're in the army. I don't understand!" Without a pause in his cadence, General DeLong added, "You will get a uniform." Knowing that further discussion would be fruitless with this "by the book" general, Joe accepted the unavoidable conclusion that he was now a uniformed captain in the United States Army Reserve with regular hours. He also was required to house himself in army accommodations, so his next task was to find quarters at Camp Murray, adjacent to Fort Lewis.

Tracking down his friend Captain Chuck Carroll who was judge advocate at Fort Lewis, Joe asked if there weren't officers' quarters available for his use. The athletically built former All-American football star said, I'll see what I can scrape together for you." He managed.

Joe now had officers' quarters on base that he could live in during the week while continuing to work at Caldwell, Lycette and Diamond on weekends as he stayed with his family in Seattle.

Concerned that the new arrangement with the army might mean that he would inevitably receive orders to transfer to some remote base, Joe began to look for another job. Once again, he called upon his friend Captain Carroll but found that there was nothing available on the post at the moment. He inquired as to who was in charge of the construction quartermasters and was told that the head man was Colonel Antonovich.

The construction quartermaster was connected with the Quartermaster Corps at the time and was in charge of all army construction including airfields, housing, office space, and just about anything else that required a hammer and nail.

Sitting across the desk from Colonel Antonovich by appointment, Joe asked if the colonel had need of a judge advocate on his staff. "As a lawyer," Joe said, "I was attorney for the Associated General Contractors as well as for the Seattle Master Builders for several years."

Seemingly unimpressed, the colonel announced, "I've been getting along fine without a judge advocate or lawyer on my staff for years and I see no need for one now." He went on, "On top of that, I wouldn't know how to get you on my staff if I *did* want you. The army doesn't operate like civilians do. I'm not able to go out and hire people without an appropriate request being made in quadruplicate."

Disappointed, Joe left the colonel's office and started down the hallway. It happened that, at that very moment, there was a bid opening going on in one of the offices with an open door. As Joe walked by, he stopped when he thought he recognized some people seated at the large table. As he glanced in, he noticed that of the approximately twenty-five contractors seated there, he knew and had worked with almost all of them.

Though not used to seeing their lawyer and friend Joe Diamond in uniform, they recognized him. When they took a short break to say hello to Joe and comment on his snappy uniform, Joe saw an opening that could not be ignored. "Gentlemen," Joe inquired, "don't you think that Colonel Antonovich could use a lawyer in his organization?" After a few hands were shaken and good-to-see-yous out of the way, Joe took his leave.

A bare week later, the phone rang on Joe's desk. It was Colonel Antonovich. "I've had trouble locating you," intoned the colonel. "I may have a place for a judge advocate after all."

With his involvement with the army construction quarter-masters barely under way, an occasion arose when Joe found himself dealing with a property in Port Angeles, on Puget Sound, that had been donated to the army by the city of Port Angeles for the purpose of building a USO facility. Joe and Colonel Antonovich visited the proposed location, which turned out to be next door to a building that Joe spotted as an obvious brothel. He pointed this out to Antonovich, who, chuckling, said, "What's wrong with that? At least it'll be convenient." Having finished their momentary mirth, Joe and Antonovich both decided it would be inappropriate for the USO to be located there. A different location would be more desirable and less embarrassing. Joe says, "I could almost picture the 20-point headlines in the local paper, 'ARMY BUILDS USO NEXT TO HOUSE OF JOY.'"

It fell to Joe to meet with the mayor of Port Angeles to arrange to successfully trade the "convenient" location for another property located a respectable distance from the bawdy house.

Later on, Joe was about to be assigned to Washington, D.C., when he heard of a Captain Fitch who was very happy in D.C. and who was about to be reassigned to the state of Washington and would be in charge of acquiring real estate here. Joe wasn't overjoyed with the prospect of leaving his family and going to D.C., and Captain Fitch wasn't jumping up and down with glee over the orders that would place him in cold, wet Seattle. After a number of phone calls and some persuading of senior officers (he was rapidly becoming a master negotiator), Joe was able to trade assignments with Fitch and remain in Seattle in a job that he was becoming quite proficient at—acquiring real estate for the army.

On a fateful Sunday, while on his office phone with another lawyer who would become a lifelong friend, Simon (Si) Wampold, trying to negotiate a settlement of a legal matter, Si said, "Wait a minute, Joe! Hold it! The radio news says the Japanese just bombed Pearl Harbor." Thinking Wampold was kidding him, Joe retorted, "Stop it, Si. We need to get this matter settled." It was December 7, 1941. Joe could hear the radio being turned up in the background at Si's office. We were at war. Now listening intently to his own radio, he heard that all military personnel were being ordered to report to their bases at once. He hurried from his office on the 20th floor of the Exchange Building to the ground floor and, in civilian clothes, tried to exit the building so he could proceed to his duty station. He was stopped dead in his tracks by representatives of the U.S. Secret Service who had sealed off the building even though only minutes had gone by since the announcement of the attack. A number of Japanese import/export companies had their offices there, and the Secret Service wasted no time in making sure, as a security measure, that no one entered or left the building. It was a mystery to Joe how they arrived almost before the fact. Apparently, suspicion of an impending attack by high government officials had put security precautions in motion days before the actual event.

It took some persuading, but Joe finally convinced the agents at the entrance that he was an army officer reporting to his unit as ordered, and he was allowed to leave. Soon after he became fully involved with the army, he received orders: Report to Fort Douglas near Salt Lake City ... yesterday! Now a major, Joe was being assigned to duty with the Judge Advocate General's office. "I wasn't very happy about it either," Joe states. With a law practice and a family to be concerned about, he called his immediate army superior in Portland, Oregon, to inquire about the new assignment and was told by the colonel in charge, "You're much too valuable to me where you are, Major Diamond. Just ignore those orders."

Joe suspected just ignoring those orders wouldn't be so easy, and noticing his old friend and school chum Captain Charles Carroll's name on the orders, he called to see what he could find out about them. "I did you a favor, Joe," reported Chuck Carroll. "The head of the Judge Advocate General's office was at Fort Lewis the other day, discussing all the judge advocates he had in his command, and I noticed that he had overlooked you. I told him all about you and what a good officer you were." "Thanks, Chuck" was Joe's somewhat disgusted response.

"I'm sorry, Joe" were the commanding officer's first words on the phone from Portland to Joe. "I did everything I could for you, but I can't get those orders canceled. You'll have to report to Fort Douglas in Salt Lake City."

For the first time in his army career, Joe would have to be away from his family because they would have to stay in Seattle. "I'll find a way to move you down there," he assured Vi.

His job at Fort Douglas was primarily to review army courts-martial. In the military, every court-martial is subject to automatic appeal. The judge advocate assigned to each case is then required to review the court record and write an opinion to recommend confirming or reversing the finding of the court-martial.

At the head of that command was Colonel White, who personally signed off on all appeal opinions by his judge advocates such as Joe. Colonel White was infamous among the judge advocates working for him. He constantly changed words and sentences to language he preferred—his language. Often the changes did not affect the meaning of the document, but he insisted upon the changes being made. As there were no tape recorders or no people to take dictation, the altered opinions had to be rewritten in longhand to be typed up later by a clerk.

Joe felt that he needed to find a way to streamline the process to avoid the time-consuming and frustrating delays in obtaining the picky colonel's approval. Then, an idea struck him. Why not use words and language that had already been approved by the colonel. So, he gathered up a number of documents that had satisfied Colonel White and began to assign

Violett Diamond volunteers during WWII

numbers to sentences used in them, ending up with a total of 300 sequentially numbered passages. He had a clerk type up this "guide" for his later reference.

Now the job was a great deal easier. As he wrote opinions of new court-martial findings, Joe simply wrote down number 7, number 39, number 237, and so forth on each paper to be submitted for final approval. The clerk had only to type up the sentences that corresponded with the numbers. The system worked.

When the colonel next called Joe to his office to complain about "incorrect language," Joe only had to show him that the language had been previously approved by him. After being shown his own language, with a wave of his hand he dismissed Joe from his illustrious presence saying, "Okay, forget it."

It wasn't long before the word got out and all of the other lawyers in the command began to use Joe's sentence-by-the-numbers system.

MEMORIES

"I vividly recall that Sunday morning, December 7, 1941, when Joe and I were discussing a case on the telephone. He was at work, as usual, and I was at home. Suddenly, I heard on the radio that Pearl Harbor had been bombed. I knew that Joe was an officer in the reserves. Immediately, he hung up the phone and rushed out to report to his outfit to do his duty. This is not only interesting from a historic standpoint, but it also typifies the chief characteristic of Joe Diamond—namely, courage. There are many other traits which could be discussed, but courage is the hallmark of his character. Regardless of circumstances, Joe has always done what he thought was right."

– Simon "Si" Wampold

"When we first met, you were a colonel and I was a lieutenant in the Army JAG Reserve Corps, and you always have been a superior officer. I have never known the privilege of being on the same side in a legal matter, nor the horror of being on the opposite side. You were kind enough to refer some professional legal matters, and in each case the matter was interesting and demanding, and was always PAID. This is real friendship between attorneys. Over the top with the best of luck, and give 'em hell."

– Thomas B. Brand

"At Fort Douglas, Utah, when I was a captain in the Judge Advocate General's Corps, Joe arrived from Seattle. He was a major, and we commiserated on the inefficient manner claims were being processed. I finally threw up my hands when the colonel sent me a claim to process

for some woman who had sent her son a cake which he claimed not to have received. She itemized the specifics of what went into the cake and sent us a claim for $1.40. I told Joe I was going to send her a letter with my $1.40 and forget the claim, but the colonel heard of this and refused permission."

– Henry Clausen

"Captain Diamond was on duty at Fort Lewis when I met him in May 1941. He and Captain Chuck Carroll were on duty prior to my assignment there as a new major. One evening before we went to dinner, I suggested we play 'odd man' pays for the dinner. Captain Carroll lost. Joe ordered two steak dinners and Chuck had a fit. He asked Joe how he could do that to an old friend? Joe very meekly replied, 'Because I'm hungry.'"

– Eugene Cushing
Retired general of the army,
Retired judge

"Back in 1938 most young lawyers and businessmen belonged to the Seattle Junior Chamber of Commerce. Joe Diamond was one of the leaders and carried a good deal of weight. He was impressive. At least he impressed me, a young lawyer. Joe and I entered the active army service at the same time, six months before Pearl Harbor. He was a captain and I, a lieutenant, so I had to salute him. At the time, we fit our uniforms very nicely. Joe had an office at Fort Lewis and made tours of inspection to Centralia and Elma, where the junior officers were doing all of the work. Often Joe was accompanied by Major Eugene C. Cushing, and he had to salute him as the senior officer present. All of this was nonsense of course, because we were *all lawyers. Anyway, Joe gave a good account of himself in the Big War, gathered a few ribbons, and retired as a colonel. Both of us like to be called "colonel" but we don't salute anymore. Joe has argued a few cases before in the two courts where I have presided. Sometimes he won."*

– Eugene A. Wright
Retired judge

CHAPTER SEVEN
ON TO WASHINGTON

In the final phone call of the many they shared while Joe was stationed in Utah, Violett informed him, "I'm driving to Utah in the morning. I will be arriving in a few days to join you." With a note of loving finality in her voice she added, "You'd better find a house for us."

Searching high and low and everywhere in between, he finally found a furnished house that could be rented. Joe had been lonely, but now he was happy. Once again he could be with his family, Vi and the two children, Joel and Diane. Things were looking up, but the Army does strange things. The very next day, he received orders to report to the Judge Advocate School in Ann Arbor, Michigan, for a six-week course in military law and related subjects. The unwelcome orders specified that he was to report in five days. This may have been one of the few times Josef said, "Damn!" Dismayed that he was to be separated from his family again, he decided to call General McNeil, who was the assistant judge advocate general in Washington, D.C.

"Sir," he started, "with my wife and family due to arrive in three days, would it be possible to put off going to that class for six weeks so that I can spend some time with my family? Perhaps I could attend the next class." "Major Diamond," retorted the general, "you are an officer in the United States Army, and you will report for duty as directed!" That was the proverbial that.

Vi and the children arrived the day Joe was to board the train for Ann Arbor. After a brief goodbye, he found himself on an eastbound train and once again missing his family. It was a travesty of timing that only an army can make.

On arrival at the school, Joe noticed a sign on the bulletin board in the headquarters office making it amply clear that families were not allowed to join their spouses (or should that be "spice"?) there. Shortly thereafter, on the phone with Vi, with him explaining the regulation, she said, "I don't care. I'm coming there anyway. Find another house for us." He who was well on his way to becoming the great persuader had not persuaded, a failure of which I feel certain he was grateful.

For days, after class, he continued looking for suitable living quarters before he finally found an old mansion in which lived one person, a widow whose husband had been killed in WWI. This massive estate home, he soon found out, had 30 rooms and four floors. In full uniform, Joe banged the heavy knocker against the door twice—shades of a Bela Lugosi movie? An old woman appeared. Apparently touched by his uniform denoting his service to his country, which must have brought back memories of her late husband, she listened respectfully as he explained his need of a place to live for six weeks, and finally, she agreed to move upstairs to the fourth floor to allow Joe and his family the run of the rest of the place until December 23, 1944, when the school was to end. She agreed further to settle for $150 rent for the short period of time but insisted that he pay the entire heating bill. An unsuspecting Joe agreed. He was soon to learn that the cost of heating that massive, drafty old building would exceed $400 a month!

Joe and his family, Joel now six years old and Diane three, finally had a place to live. During his spare time, they all enjoyed sledding on the picturesque snow-draped hills in the area.

Upon graduation, Joe and family set out for Washington, D.C., as he had orders to report to the Judge Advocate General's headquarters there. They were successful in finding living quarters fairly quickly and began to settle into a daily routine.

Reporting for duty, Joe was invited (in the army, the word "invited" means "ordered") to attend a reception being held in the same building in which his office was located. There were many more pleasant ways he could envision to spend that day, but he obliged by wending his way through a long, slow reception line to be introduced to the judge advocate general and the assistant JAG, General McNeil.

Violett Diamond with Joel and Diane

"Haven't we met before?" General McNeil asked. "No, sir, we haven't" was the reply. "Aren't you the young man who called to say you couldn't report for duty at the law school in Ann Arbor and asked for a six-week delay?" the general parried. Embarrassed, Joe answered, "Yes, sir." "Well … I see you made it." The general smugly chuckled.

After working in that office for just a week, Joe was summoned to appear before General Cramer, the judge advocate general with four stars on his collar. From behind his oversize oak desk (it seemed large enough to provide a tempting emergency landing field for a small plane in distress) General Cramer began, "Major Diamond, in addition to your present duties, I want you to take on the responsibility for tax matters affecting construction contracts in the western states. What with you being from the West Coast, I thought you might appreciate the opportunity to get out there once in a while to interview the various heads of the tax sections there." Joe was having a hard time containing himself. Even considering that he had little if any athletic ability in gymnastics, he would have offered to do handstands for the assignment.

The general continued, "Also, I remember receiving a letter from you when you were with the construction quartermaster at Fort Lewis involving taxes in connection with a construction project. It was very well done. I was impressed that you definitely knew your subject." "I would be happy to take on the West Coast responsibilities, sir," Joe agreed, barely able to contain his enthusiasm.

One of his early West Coast assignments had to do with the Boeing Company, headquartered in Seattle. The company had a contract to build war planes for the Army Air Corps (later to become the U.S. Air Force) and they were being charged an onerous B & O (business and occupations) tax by the city of Seattle. As the contract was on a "cost plus" basis, the tax was being charged back to the government.

Beginning to poke into the matter, Joe soon discovered that the Boeing plant was located half in and half out of the city limits of Seattle. It seemed to him that Boeing should be required to pay only half of the amount currently being assessed against them. He discussed the matter with Boeing's president but met with resistance there. The Boeing executive was concerned that, once the war was over, the city of Seattle might eventually make claim for payment of back taxes and the company would have to take a disastrous financial hit. With no encouragement from Boeing, Joe decided to put on a one-man front against the city of Seattle.

Meeting with the Seattle City Council, Joe made his case and, after an exhausting several hours of presentation of precedent and common sense, prevailed. The B & O tax was reduced by half. Though Boeing's hierarchy wasn't happy with the effort (after all, the extra tax burden was no skin off their nose), the federal government was greatly pleased that the savings would amount to many millions of dollars. It might be well to add here that Boeing never did have to pay any "back taxes" as a result of Joe's pleadings.

Back in D.C. and continuing his duties there, a few months went by when, once again, he was called into General Cramer's presence in his opulent office. "Major Diamond," the general's conversation began, "I want you to report to the Corps of Engineers and assist Colonel Straight with construction contract matters. Colonel Straight is also a judge advocate officer," the general continued, "and he's going to be released for an overseas assignment. Since you're familiar with construction, Major, you are our man for the job."

"I'd much rather stay on board here, General," Joe responded. "I'm pleased that I'm able to return to the Pacific Coast once in a while to handle tax matters there." "Well then, Major," announced the general, "I'll give you a double assignment. You will continue to handle the West Coast tax matters in addition to taking over the legal department when Colonel Straight leaves." With just the slightest hint of sarcasm (one does not get sarcastic with a general whose highly polished four stars are reflecting the overhead light brilliantly) Joe added, "That's very generous, sir, but I'd rather stay right here."

"Unfortunately," commanded the grim-faced general, "we don't have anyone else who can handle the job. You're the only one available who can do it." He quickly added, "But, I don't know how the Corps of Engineers will treat a major, so I'm promoting you to lieutenant colonel before you report there." Orders are orders, and a promotion is a promotion. Joe saluted and departed.

The military title *colonel* is one of great weight. It is one of those titles like *general* or *judge* or *governor* that, out of courtesy, should be used when addressing that person for the rest of his or her life. Albeit in some of our southern states the integrity of the title is sorely tested as it is frequently and carelessly adopted by anyone who has more than three dollars and seventy five cents in the bank whether or not that person ever served in the Boy Scouts, much less the army. Nonetheless, attaining the rank of colonel in the United States Army is of no small consequence and carries with it the required, but not always earned, respect of junior officers, along with their snappier salute. It also carries a much greater responsibility for the actions of large numbers of army personnel. Army-wise, Joe had arrived.

There was much to learn about his new duties before Colonel Straight departed for his new assignment. The Corps of Engineers was responsible for all army construction such as airfields, hangars, barracks for the troops, and the all-important mess hall. They were also responsible for all purchases of equipment to facilitate construction. Trucks, bulldozers, wrecking balls, and road graders were also among the items the corps dealt with on a frequent basis. With his background of handling construction contracts back in Puget Sound country, Joe caught on more quickly than even he expected to.

With his office in a newly constructed facility called the New War Department Building, Joe reveled in his comfortable, air-conditioned space. The building had become "necessary" when the war broke out because the army considered the previous space too small to accommodate the War Department (now the Department of Defense). The building was more luxurious than any army facility to which he had been previously assigned, in Joe's opinion.

Almost immediately a problem arose having to do with a contract Ford Motor Company had to build tanks for the army. Though Ford had agreed to the contract more than a year earlier, not a single tank had rolled off their production line thus far. It was 1945 and the war was expected to end soon. Not only in Europe but in the Pacific as well, our foes were showing signs of weakening, and the conclusion of both conflicts was in sight. Because Ford would, at best, produce their first tank not long before victory was realized, it became clear that the contract would have to be canceled. A review of the contract revealed that it was another one of those "cost plus" agreements. Considering that the army had already paid for the construction of 25 miles of highway at Ford's River Rouge plant and had substantially remodeled several buildings, trying to work out a reasonable settlement was a formidable task for Colonels Straight and Diamond.

The pair of colonels attempted to secure financial information from Ford Motor Company on how much money Ford had expended to date on preparing to build the tanks. A veritable bevy of Ford Motor Company vice presidents quoted some astronomical figures as to how much they had spent thus far on the tank contract, but they had had no paper work to back up their claims because the company kept no separate records by department. When Henry Ford was setting up his horse-less carriage business, he simply decided that whatever income was derived would be used to pay expenses and anything left over belonged to the company. Simple but impossible to work with, so far as Joe was concerned, in trying to determine a fair settlement with them.

After three days in Detroit, dealing with two senior vice presidents, a settlement was finally reached, which provided that Ford would be given all of the improvements at the River Rouge plant and an additional one-million-dollar payment. The settlement seemed to satisfy everyone concerned even though there was no real basis to determine what the auto manufacturer should be paid. Joe felt that it was a good settlement from the government's standpoint as it put to rest any possibility of a protracted litigation which could go on for years and cost multiple millions of dollars to be borne by the tax payers.

Some years later, a couple of identically dressed, gray-suited agents from the Federal Bureau of Investigation presented themselves in Joe's office. They quickly came to the point of their visit when one demanded, "We want to know about the settlement you made for one million dollars to Ford Motor Company. Do you remember that?"

Joe thought for a moment. Though he had handled many contract disputes, settlements, and problems for the army, he couldn't forget that one. It was unique. "Of course I remember," he replied. "That was the best settlement I could make at the time since there was no basis in fact for the payment. I did it to avoid any further litigation."

"What kind of litigation?" one of the agents smugly asked with a strain of suspicion in his voice that was unmistakable.

"While I was with the Corps of Engineers," Joe replied, "a similar case came to my attention. It involved a lawsuit by Bethlehem Steel against the United States government that had arisen during World War I and was still going on." The two agents listened in amazement. "The case involved many millions of dollars over steel procurement," Joe continued, "and during my time there, we finally settled it to avoid more years of litigation at great expense to the government." He went on, "The case had gone to the United States Supreme Court at least once, and the legal bills and costs were extensive. That could easily have happened with the Ford Motor Company matter if I hadn't nipped it in the bud."

Without another word, one of the agents pulled out his little black book, made a quick note, and snapped it shut. The other said, "Thank you for your time, Mr. Diamond," and they left his office looking much less official and accusatory than when they arrived. Joe never heard from the FBI again on the matter.

Back to the army. After Colonel Straight left, Joe succeeded him in the law department, where he reported to Lieutenant General Gene Reybold, who was the chief of engineers. "Colonel Diamond," began the general, "I don't know anything about the law, and I assume you don't know anything about the engineering department."

"That's right, sir," Joe admitted. To use an old navy term, he liked the cut of this general's jib.

"So I won't be bothering you with the law, and you won't bother me with engineering. You'll be assuming all responsibility for the legal department of the corps." Joe was pleased. It was quickly established that he would run the law office to his own satisfaction without having to answer to anyone about its operation. In his new position, he guessed he would be made privy to many sensitive and highly confidential documents having to do with the war. How wrong he was! Most of his meetings, arranged by top brass, were motivational by nature, and many were designed to be of assistance to the American Red Cross in seeking contributions. A determined officer, Joe wasn't exactly elated over this turn of events. All that was about to change.

As head of the Army Service Command, General Sommerville was General Reybold's superior officer. Sommerville, the commanding general, ordered Reybold to build a highway from the Mexican border, all the way through Mexico, through the Central American countries to culminate at the Panama Canal. The War Department wanted to protect itself against a sneak attack and invasion from the canal as it had experienced in Pearl Harbor. They wanted quick access to the area to defend it without undue delay.

The undertaking required that train loads of machinery and equipment that had been used in the building of an airfield in Canada be shipped via rail to the Mexican border. Human error, as it often does, entered the project. Somebody who was supposed to ready this equipment for loading on the train neglected to drain the radiators of the various vehicles being shipped. Traveling through Canada and the Northwest during the icy-cold winter months caused radiators and engine blocks to burst. Piles of money and many weeks of repair to make the machinery serviceable were expended. But that wasn't the worst of it. The worst part was that the media became aware of the blunder.

As soon as it became public knowledge that the army was building a road from the Mexican border to the Panama Canal, a hue and cry arose as it often does by the Monday morning quarterbacks about the "waste of money which would be better spent on fighting equipment to win the war."

One of the top radio announcers of the time, Fulton Lewis, began to broadcast derogatory accounts of the Corps of Engineers' Pan-American Highway project. After interviewing some lowly clerk, probably a malcontent, he made accusations of waste and corruption. He put forth his opinion that the project was not only superfluous but would never be finished before war's end.

After weeks of such radio accusations, General Reybold got together with Joe to discuss the matter. "What can I do to stop Lewis from making these irresponsible comments on the radio?" he inquired. "Nothing," Joe responded. "The best thing to do is to ignore him." "That doesn't sound like a good plan, Joe," replied Reybold. "Instead, I want him to come in to my office and have a talk with me."

Very concerned, Joe advised, "That would probably be the worst thing you can do, General. Whatever you say, he'll twist it around and make more headlines in doing so." "Well, regardless, I should speak to him and stop these baseless rumors," the general insisted.

Not long after, Joe heard a Fulton Lewis broadcast where he said he had met with General Reybold at the general's request and then branched off into another tirade of derogatory and inaccurate comments. Joe wished to himself that the general had taken his advice and not given the anti-army broadcaster more ammunition for verbal attack.

Due to the notoriety, the affair went all the way up the army's chain of command. Finally, the United States Senate set up a committee headed up by Senator Harry Truman to investigate the allegations of racketeering and waste in the highway project.

In the meantime, being out of the immediate loop, Joe had managed to arrange for a weeklong furlough. By special arrangement with the navy, which had a hotel in Virginia specifically set aside for military personnel to rest and recuperate, Joe and his family drove all day long to get to Norfolk for the much-looked-forward-to break.

That evening, he received a frantic phone call from General Reybold. "I need you to come back to Washington and appear before the Truman committee," the general pleaded. "I'm being investigated, and I want you to represent me at those hearings."

"It's impossible for me to get back in time for the hearings, sir," Joe answered, to which the general quickly replied, "My private plane is already on its way down. It will pick you up at the airfield at 0500 tomorrow and bring you back here." Disgusted at the timing of these events but respectful of the difficult situation the general faced, Joe thought, "So much for a vacation!" Early the next day, he reluctantly flew back to the capitol, leaving Vi and the two kids behind at the free hotel to enjoy a few days that they had hoped to spend with him.

Joe arrived in time for the first day of hearings only to find out that the committee had already subpoenaed and received truckloads of records from the Corps of Engineers, which they were in process of reviewing. Preparing to represent Reybold, Joe suggested to the general that it be made clear, early on, that the Pan-American Highway was General Sommerville's project and that Sommerville's representatives should have to make the case for the necessity of the highway for the war effort.

"That's not the way this is going to happen, Joe," the general indignantly replied. "I'm taking full responsibility for the construction of the highway and the justification of the expenses."

That is the way the hearing went for a full ten days. General Reybold took the blame for what the media had labeled the "highway fiasco." He was the subject of much innuendo about graft, corruption, and costly mistakes. After no evidence surfaced detrimental to General Reybold from the

Truman committee's hearings, the Pan-American Highway resumed construction. It was a slow process and was never completed as intended by those very senior but very silent officers who had drawn up its plans.

Joe learned something during the development of and hearings about this project. He learned about taking responsibility for one's actions. He greatly respected General Reybold for taking the heat on the highway project even though he was only following orders and was not directly responsible. This was a lesson that Joe would commit to his own life, and it would garner much respect from his clients and peers.

MEMORIES

"I was seven or eight years old when I first met Joe Diamond. Joe was in his officer's uniform. He was very dashing and impressive. He and Vi were good friends of my parents in those days. I recall when Diane was born.

"The good news was, he gave me a job in his parking lots when I was going to law school. The bad news was, he would inspect every Saturday morning and have us all picking up, cleaning, and scrubbing up—military style. When I grew a mustache in the '50s he told me he didn't like it and to shave it off. I told him that I had seen his law school graduation picture and he had a mustache. He said, 'Yes but I looked distinguished … you look like a hippy.' Joe got me my first law job, as an assistant U.S. attorney. He came to my office one day and looked around for a minute or two and said, 'Your office is bigger than mine.'

"Joe has had dozens and dozens of people he has watched over and helped over the years. I am lucky to have been one of them.

"Joe's worst quality—you simply can't get him to say anything bad about anyone. Joe's second worst quality—he is always criticizing my dress and Gary Gayton's [another well-known Seattle lawyer] dress, especially our ties. Yet, if Muriel didn't coordinate him every morning, he'd come to work looking like he was trying out for a part in a movie about Damon Runyon."

— Ron Neubauer
Prominent Seattle attorney

"I first met Joe when I was a young attorney with Diamond & Sylvester, a growing midsize law firm in Seattle. Diamond & Sylvester had occupied its office in the Hoge Building on the corner of Second and Cherry for approximately 40 years.

"Joe's office was at the end of the hall in the corner of the building. The office had windows on two sides. Outside the windows was a wide cornice, or ledge, intended as a decorative ring around the building. The ledge was home to many pigeons and seagulls.

"Joe, always wanting to make friends, would often lift open his window and feed bread to the seagulls. Joe and the seagulls got to know each other quite well. Oftentimes the seagulls, when they hadn't been fed, or felt that they had not been fed enough, would screech loudly outside Joe's window. If their desire for the bread was sufficient, they would not only make that loud racket but would also pound on Joe's window with their beaks and flap their wings.

"There was many a time in Joe's office in the Hoge Building when meetings regarding the fate of large properties or businesses in Seattle or in the nation had to be interrupted so that Joe could appease his pecking, flapping, screeching friends on the ledge outside.

"And that reminds me of my favorite story about Josef that I was a part of: While on a business trip to Phoenix, Arizona, I received a phone call from Joe. 'There is someone I want you to meet while you are down in Phoenix,' Joe said. 'There is this woman I have been seeing, and she is not just another date.'

"Well, as you might have guessed, the woman was the lovely Muriel. I met her after one of her performances and had a wonderful and engaging luncheon. During that luncheon she told me, 'You know, Joe and I are engaged to be married.' I had to admit that Joe had not yet told me about the marriage plans. 'I would not doubt that a bit,' she said. 'I have told all of my friends in Chicago, but I don't think Joe is telling people in Seattle.'

"Sure enough, Joe had kept Seattle in the dark about his plans. 'I know I have to spread the word,' Joe said. 'I can't have my friends in Seattle hear it from those in Chicago.'"

– Robert Hibbs
Another Seattle lawyer

CHAPTER EIGHT
WAR NEARING AN END

With the war in Europe over and the war in the Pacific winding down, the lure of leaving active duty in the army loomed ever larger for Joe.

It was August 1945. Germany had surrendered to United States and Allied forces. Joe was aware, because of his position, that another branch had been set up within the Corps of Engineers—the Manhattan District. The commanding General of the new group had, among others, General Reybold under his command. When Joe asked his general what the Manhattan District was doing, Reybold said he didn't know. Seemingly, no one knew what the secretive branch was up to. No one knew that the Manhattan District was part of the Manhattan Project, nor did anyone know that there was such a thing as the Manhattan Project. One of Joe's friends, another general, furtively informed Joe that "Something unusual is going to happen in three or four days." It happened. Hiroshima and Nagasaki were flattened by atomic bombs, and thousands upon thousands died. Soon, Japan surrendered, and World War II, including the war in the Pacific, was over.

Joe's boss, General Reybold, was soon to retire and had been hired to build a bridge across the Delaware River. Joe thought that would be a good time for him to depart the army too and suggested to the general that he should be released at the same time the general was. Reybold pointed out that he had a problem: he couldn't take the bridge-building job because he hadn't used all of his furlough time and couldn't officially leave the army until he had. In a strange twist that only the army could dream up, he could leave physically but had to sit around and wait for his six months' furlough time to be used up before he could accept the bridge-building job because normal procedure dictated that he couldn't draw army pay and state pay at the same time.

"What if I could find a way so you could draw both pays at the same time? Would you let me out when you get out?" Joe asked. "Can't be done," the general said with a note of finality in his voice. "It's not legal." "Just because it hasn't been done yet doesn't make it illegal, General," responded Joe.

Convinced that it couldn't be done, the general agreed that if Joe could arrange for him to be able to take the bridge-building job, he would see to it that Joe got off active duty when the general left. Anxious to work out any problems so that the general could accept his new job and depart the army, Joe and his friend Lt. Jesse Wolff spent the next two days pouring over case histories in the library. Not finding any specific precedent either for or against being paid by the two entities, Joe and Lt. Wolff drew up an opinion that would permit General Reybold to take his new job while drawing pay for his unused furlough time. Joe presented this opinion to General Cramer for his approval. The general said it couldn't be done. Joe confidently asserted, "Since I can't find any law that would prevent it, it isn't illegal. Therefore, it must be legal." He made the argument that General Cramer could make it a new law by simply signing his approval on the opinion. The general objected, saying that the controller general (the top military lawyer in the country, who reviewed everything coming out of the Judge Advocate General's office) would never agree to it, but Joe countered, "What if I promise not to let the document with your signature out of my possession until it is agreed to by the controller general?" You may have detected that Joe (now a "bird colonel") really wanted out of the army and back into his law office in Seattle.

General Cramer reluctantly agreed and signed the document with that promise and understanding. Then, it was off to the office of the controller general (another gent with three stars on his epaulets) for his signature. He too said there was no law to support the opinion. "Yes, sir," said a determined Joe, "that is correct, but just because there is no law in support of it doesn't mean it isn't legal. You're the top lawyer in the country—you can make it law by simply signing it." The general said he needed to think about it and added, "Let me take the letter with me to study it." Joe explained that he couldn't release the paper but suggested that since the general knew its contents, he should be able to consider it without having it in hand. With an air of resignation, the controller general signed the document and sent Joe on his way.

Colonel Joe now had a document allowing General Reybold to leave his command and take the bridge-building job without having to wait for his six months of furlough to be used up, and it was signed by the judge advocate general and the controller general. Civilian life was looking ever nearer.

Joe presented the signed document to General Reybold and asked, "Now will you cut orders so that I can get out of the army at the same time you do?" The general's response wasn't pleasing to Joe. "No, I'm not going to let you out. They need you around here." Joe reminded him of his promise, and soon orders were cut. Joe left active duty with the army and returned to Seattle.

Before war had broken out, Joe's older brother, Louis, was experiencing great success in expanding his Diamond Parking operations. He had managed to build the business up to 17 thriving locations in Seattle. But as the old saying goes, "Every silver lining has a dark cloud behind it" (or something like that). As the war progressed, it became more and more difficult to find responsible employees to attend his parking locations and deliver gas to customers. All the good men were going off to war, whether willingly or otherwise. There were a very few available men, and those usually became noticeably unreliable immediately following the delivery of a pay-check. Winos and derelicts were about all there was in the potential workforce.

Joe commented just recently, "We didn't know how to operate without attendants then. I'm not sure we know how to now."

Toward the end of the war, the shortage of good help caused Louis to reduce his locations to just four. He had, however, made some very wise investments in real estate on First Hill (Joe had helped as his army obligation permitted) and had built three "medical centers." They were large single-story buildings with offices built to suit and leased to doctors. They were called the Seattle Medical Center, Madison Medical Center, and Broadway Medical Center.

As the end of the war appeared imminent, Louis contacted brother Josef and explained that he and his wife, Dorothy, were tired of the parking business and were going to retire and move to Hawaii as his monthly income from his medical centers was quite satisfactory. He told Joe of his intent to close down the parking business unless Joe wanted to continue it upon his separation from the army. Joe said he would like to take over that business, so Louis agreed to keep it open until Joe returned to Seattle.

And the rest is history.

MEMORIES

"My association with Josef began when he was a legal assistant to Hugh Caldwell in the late 1920s. Hugh was mayor of Seattle, and I was with the Arctic Fur Company. After the war, when my cantankerous associate J. D. Simpson had withdrawn our legal work from Caldwell, Lycette and Diamond, Josef confronted Simpson and demanded his right, as a returning veteran, to get his job back. He was successful and represented Arctic Furs and me continuously since the mid-1940s."

– Mel and Johanna Steil

"Joe was a very good army officer," noted General C. E. "Red" Straight, *"who did a good job for the Corps of Engineers and for me."*

"There has never been a more decent and honorable person than Joe Diamond. When the wolves howled, the jackals screeched, and the donkeys brayed, Joe did not join them."

– Michael P. Stern

"When Colonel Josef Diamond interviewed me for a position in the new unit, which he was heading up for the Corps of Engineers, after a fairly short time he said, in effect, 'I guess you'll do.' We ended up working together until the end of World War II. Never once did he exercise his privilege of rank as a field grade officer over this lowly second lieutenant or over any of his junior officers. He just ran a very good law firm, acting like a senior partner in a firm with only one client. When the war was over, of course almost everyone was eager to return to civilian life, but some regulations had been established to

govern the timing and sequence of releases. Since I had spent many months overseas, my release date was early. Colonel Diamond, however, was lamenting to me the fact that it would be some months before his release date came up. So, he asked me to look into the matter to see if there might be anything in the president's executive order which would enable him to exit more quickly. Eventually, we did find a way, and I was very happy to have played a small part in that—a very small part for a very deserving gentleman."

– Jesse D. Wolff
Attorney

"Joe was my warm friend during our days in service at Fort Douglas and Washington.

"When Joe moved into housing quarters assigned him in Washington, he phoned and invited me and my wife over. When we arrived we found them living in a ramshackle, broken-down house, with steps leading up to it so rickety that we went around to the back rather than trust the stairs. I asked Joe if he wanted a contribution for his living expenses, and the whole thing was a big laugh with us.

"I considered him superior as an army officer and a positive genius at simplifying what would otherwise be most complex. His wife was always a delightful and charming addition to our group."

– Henry C. Clausen

38-year-old Colonel Josef Diamond being presented Legion of Merit medal

West Seattle Herald
Feb. 14, 1946

Col. Josef Diamond, Seattle attorney of 6355 Beach Drive, received the congratulations of Col. Conrad P. Hardy, Seattle District Engineer, who present-ed Diamond with the Legion of Merit medal Wednesday, Feb. 6, for services rendered the office, Chief of Engineers, Washington, D.C., between January 3, 1944 and September 28, 1945. Colonel Hardy represented Brig. Gen. Philip Bruton, Pacific Division Engineer of San Francisco in presentation of the award for outstanding contribu-tions in formulating legal procedures for the Corps of Engineers' war construction, on military supply and contracting programs.

CHAPTER NINE
LAW AND PARKING

Back in Seattle early in 1946, Joe was welcomed back to his law firm, which had moved from the Exchange Building to the eighth floor of the Hoge Building, and he resumed his duties there. When he left to fulfill his army obligation, the firm name had been Caldwell, Lycette and Diamond but the name now was Lycette, Diamond and Sylvester. Since Hugh Caldwell had left Seattle and a longtime lawyer, Jack Sylvester, had joined the firm as a partner, the name had changed. At the same time, Joe took over the operation of Diamond Parking and its four remaining parking lots from his brother, Louis as he had agreed to do. His work was cut out for him. Fortunately, Joe's younger brother, Leon, who owned three service stations in town, merged with him and together they began to build and run Diamond Parking.

With most of the soldiers, sailors, marines, and fliers not yet separated from their military units, Joe had the same problem that his brother had suffered with—limited available, employable people to look after the parking locations. With need being the parent of innovation, Joe came up with what was then a unique plan to solve the labor problem. He created a slotted coin box that allowed parking customers to drop their money into the box and go about their business. This concept was noted and copied by competitors in the parking business. Soon coin boxes began cropping up on parking lots throughout the Seattle area and across the country.

The first few weeks back in the saddle were difficult. After a long time dealing with military law and with civilian law having been in a constant state of change, as it has been throughout history, Joe worked long hours to catch up with his colleagues in the field of law. Much time was also dedicated to reestablishing himself with loyal clients from days of yore. Many of the clients who welcomed him back with open arms were construction contractors who appreciated the additional knowledge of construction legal matters he had picked up with the Corps of Engineers.

Once again Joe was representing the Seattle Master Builder's Association, whose membership was mostly made up of residential builders. He also reestablished himself with a previous client, the Association of General Contractors, who were commercial builders for the most part. With these clients and many others back in the fold, Joe's client list began to flourish. He had been, before the war, a very successful lawyer. Now with new homes and businesses in a boom period, his success and, frankly, his bank account were magnified many times. I mention his bank account for a good reason. In the 43 years, thus far, that I have known and worked with Joe Diamond, he always used his financial strength to invest in a diverse collection of businesses. I watched him take on businesses that were in dire straits and turn them around, almost always with a 50/50 partner. The challenge was his motivation; profit was always secondary but often was the result.

Even though still comparatively young, Colonel Diamond was rapidly becoming one of the best-known and highly respected lawyers in the area.

Throughout his career, Joe had shied away from defending people in criminal matters. He always said that he felt the need to like the people he represented. He wanted his clients to be his friends as well as clients. He expected them to be the kind of friends he could invite over for dinner with his family. He felt he would have difficulty liking the kind of person who is caught up in a criminal prosecution. "Most of them are guilty or they wouldn't be a defendant in a criminal cause," he explained, "and I certainly wouldn't want that kind of person in my house for dinner with my wife and my children."

Sometimes it just didn't work that way. Take the time when a friend and longtime client in Alaska and the owner of a company, along with his superintendent, were accused of arson when his building had burned to the ground. An investigation showed that the business had been losing money and evidence seemed to indicate the guilt of Joe's friend, bringing about the charge of arson. Because the alleged crime had been committed prior to Alaska becoming the 49th state, the case was tried in federal court in Alaska.

The accused friend convinced Joe that he was innocent and needed to be represented in this very serious matter. Joe reluctantly agreed and traveled to Alaska to defend the man. As the story developed, it became even more serious. There had been an apartment on an upper floor of the late business that had been occupied by two people, who barely escaped the inferno with their lives and, fortunately, only minor injuries. After three days of trial, the charges against the superintendent were dismissed on grounds of insufficient evidence, but the battle went downhill from there.

The prosecution trotted out a witness who had worked for the company and who testified that he had been paid by the superintendent on orders from the owner (Joe's client), to pour the gasoline and scratch the match that started the blaze. The witness had been granted immunity to come forward and testify. As a side note, it seems to me a little unfair that the prosecution (government) can legally bribe a witness, as in this case, but if defense were to do so, they'd likely be fined heavily and probably spend some time looking at striped daylight from the inside of a government accommodation. But I digress.

Joe was able to weaken the witness's testimony somewhat, but there was still a boxcar load of evidence against his client that would have to be overcome. And Joe was beginning to have serious doubts as to his client's innocence. At the adjournment of the court one day, Joe returned to his small hotel, bothered by what he suspected was a lost cause and a guilty friend and client.

Sleeping fitfully that night, Joe awakened at four o'clock in the morning to a knock on his door. After verifying the person on the other side was his client, he allowed him to enter the room. Within moments, his friend was showing great remorse and admitting his guilt. He had indeed paid to have the failing business burned down with intent to collect on the insurance policy.

When the gavel came down later that morning, Joe was faced with a dilemma. He was obligated to try to prove to the satisfaction of the court that his client was innocent even though he now knew he was guilty. He gave it his best effort, though his heart wasn't in it. His client lost and was convicted. Joe was pleased to have lost the case.

During those postwar years, the parking operation under the guidance of Leon, the company president, and Josef, its secretary, and a carefully selected group of dedicated employees grew at an exciting rate. Soon expansion spread beyond Seattle to eventually include over 1,000 garages and parking lots in nine states. Diamond Parking locations can be found now in Washington, Oregon, Utah, Alaska, Idaho, Montana, Arizona, California, and Hawaii. Much of the success of

Diamond Parking, which, according to Joe Diamond, is the oldest parking operation in the world under the same ownership as when it began, is attributable to Joe's longtime philosophy: "Any business can be a good business if you have good people. Any business will be a bad business if you have bad people."

Joe was one of the founding fathers of the National Parking Association, where he served on the board of directors from 1950 to 1975. He also served as president of that well-known organization for a period of two years. He became friends with many parking operators in the United States as well as parts of Europe through his association with the NPA. Many of the innovations that are now commonplace throughout the parking industry here and abroad were conceived and put into effect by Diamond Parking. Such things as coin boxes (they're now folding money boxes) for unmanned lots were, as earlier noted, a Diamond Parking first.

MEMORIES

"I am proud to be numbered among Joe's friends," wrote D. M. Carothers of Allright Parking, a major competitor of Diamond Parking. "When the National Parking Association was just getting off the ground, I was a foot dragger, while Joe was right up in the front ranks helping to get the fledgling organization off the ground. I am glad Joe persisted because now I am proud of my membership in the NPA. It also helped me get acquainted with Joe Diamond, and for that I am thankful."

"Beyond his abilities in construction claims arising out of his experience with the Corps of Engineers and my involvement with him in forming the Northwest Bank in 1964, I have many, many favorite stories about Joe. They all reveal him as a good friend, a credit to the community, a high example to his profession, and a man of complete integrity and honesty. His philosophy in life has always been one of getting and trying to conclude every deal or problem amicably."

– Norman E. Berg

"Back in 1954," wrote Jerry Costacos, well-known landlord in downtown Seattle and parking operator as well as one-time owner of the Airways Car Rental System, "when I arrived at my first parking association meeting, I was scared of Josef. But as the years went on and our relationship grew, he has become almost like a relative. Negotiating to buy into Budget Rent A Car, I was at Josef's office with my attorney and CPA. At one point during our discussions, my lawyer told Josef that he was going to advise me to not go through with the deal as it was written. 'If Jerry Costacos was my client,' Josef said, 'I too, would advise him not to sign this agreement. However, there is an aspect of trust that is not spelled out in the agreement, which Jerry, John Cain, and I have that will make the agreement work.' And it was to be. It worked for all three parties, in spite of my counsel's advice, which I did respect."

Paul Cressman, fellow lawyer and partner in the prestigious law firm of Short, Cressman and Burgess, where Joe was of counsel later in his life, wrote, "Joe had a fantastic reputation in the construction industry because of, among other things, his World War II record. We had sev-

eral legal matters where he was on one side and my firm was on the other. I was impressed with the way he conducted himself. Joe was always a lawyer I could call at 6:30 in the evening and he would still be in his office."

"I remember well the first time I met Colonel Josef Diamond, in 1955. I had gone to his law office to interview for a job. My legal experience was limited, but I wanted, more than anything, to be a legal secretary. That was my dream. Mr. Sylvester was talking to me, and then the door opened and there stood Colonel Josef Diamond with a big smile on his face. He said, 'Well, I don't have to go to Guatemala today after all. I was able to get Don out of jail.' I later learned that the natives had been chasing 'Don' down the beach, brandishing their rifles. That was the beginning of a friendship which has lasted 35 years, as well as a working alliance almost that long. I am still impressed that Josef almost always seemed to win. He always had a vision—the ability of seeing beyond the printed words in the law books. He would often say to one of his partners, 'But, Lyle, that can't be right. It should be this way or that way.' To this day, Josef Diamond is still one of the most influential people in my life. A giant among men."

– Beryl Ryall
Longtime legal secretary
and right arm to Joe Diamond
[She died not long after writing this.]

Meredith "Mert" Sweeting, one of the original employees of Diamond Parking, wrote, "I was a new employee of only about two weeks when Mr. Diamond came to my parking lot location still in military uniform. He complimented me on being courteous to him and said that he liked the way this lot was being run. When I was made a supervisor and attended my first supervision meeting, he impressed upon me the importance of being honest and loyal. I stayed with him for 31 years."

THURSDAY, AUGUST 31, 1995

An empire of blacktop Diamonds

Seattle lawyer Josef Diamond, self-proclaimed father of the self-serve parking lot, built his immigrant family's business into a thriving dynasty of asphalt and coin boxes.

Peter Haley/The News Tribune

Attorney and parking lot czar Josef Diamond takes care of business in his downtown Seattle office.

CHAPTER TEN
STRANGER THAN FICTION

In over 70 years of practicing law, Joe has come across some cases that even the writers of the Perry Mason books would have had trouble conjuring up.

One comes to mind that involved two of his friends in the construction business. For the purposes of this story, we'll simply call them Dick and Pete. Working well together for some years, the pair took on another partner (we shall call him Errol—the choice of name shall become evident shortly) to help them handle some large construction projects in Alaska. Mistake! It didn't take them long to conclude that their new associate was not pulling his weight. As a matter of fact, Errol was accomplishing precisely nothing, while always managing to show up on time to collect his unearned salary.

It didn't take J. Paul Getty to figure out that his drawing of a salary identical to the other two was an unnecessary drain on company funds. They fired him forthwith! Although he remained a partner, he was no longer drawing a salary.

As one might expect, Errol didn't take too kindly to his income being curtailed. The loss of money hurt him more than being fired. The predictable result was that he filed a lawsuit against Dick and Pete. Enter Joe Diamond.

When the case went to trial in King County Court in downtown Seattle, where the corporate headquarters of the company was located, Joe's job was to prove to the court that Errol wasn't earning his money and that Dick and Pete were justified in terminating his employment, even though he was still a partner in the firm.

Having done some fairly extensive research on the disgruntled Errol's activities while away from home and in Alaska, Joe decided to put the plaintiff, Errol, on the stand.

"Do you swear to tell the truth, the whole truth, and nothing but the truth so help you God?" the bailiff intoned. "I do."

"While you were in your hotel room in Alaska," Joe began, "do you recall the time—about four in the morning—when someone knocked on the door?" He continued, "And when you answered the door you found your wife standing there?" "Well … uhhh … yeah," Errol answered after several moments during which he seemed to have some difficulty recalling the incident.

"Isn't it true that at the time you had a girlfriend in the bed behind you?" Strangely, Errol's lawyer remained seated. With a flushed face, Errol answered, "Uhh, yeah." "And what did your wife do then?" inquired Joe. Errol said he couldn't recall.

"Oh, I think you remember," Joe challenged. "Your wife pulled out a .22 caliber revolver and pointed it at you, didn't she?" "Well ... yes," the plaintiff responded after a noticeable pause. "Now, when she pulled out that gun, she pointed it right at your face, correct?" Before Errol had a chance to respond, Joe went on, "And she was only six or eight inches away?" "Uhh ... yeah" came the familiar response. "And she pulled the trigger—"

Before Joe had a chance to finish the question, the plaintiff's attorney finally jumped to his feet. "Objection! What does this have to do with the lawsuit?" he inquired of the judge. "Sustained" was the judge's ruling.

Ultimately, with Joe offering arguments less titillating, the judge ruled in favor of Joe's clients. His friends Dick and Pete had won. Taking the judgment into the judge's chambers later for signature, the bailiff was instructed, "Before I sign this, I want to see Joe Diamond." Dismissed from his honor's presence, the bailiff invited Joe, by phone, to visit the judge in his chambers.

"Sit down a minute," Judge McDonald invited Joe. "I want to talk with you. During the trial in which your clients Dick and Pete were defendants," the judge asked, "you said that Errol's wife pulled the trigger?" "That's right," answered Joe. "I'm kind of sorry I had to sustain the objection that the questioning was not material to the issues," the judge went on, "because I wanted to hear the rest of the story. What happened?"

"Well, Judge," Joe explained, "when he saw his wife at the door and with a gun, Errol was so startled that his mouth dropped open. His wife pulled the trigger at that moment, and the bullet went through his open mouth and out the back of his neck, but it didn't hit anything vital." Now it was the judge's turn for his mouth to drop open. "Of course they took him to the hospital," continued Josef, "but three or four days later he was out and running around again."

"Were any charges filed against her?" asked the judge. "Her husband never filed any against her, Judge," Joe replied. "He was in too much trouble already."

And even stranger? How about the trial without a judge? As Joe was about to head out to lunch one day, his secretary told him that a man had just arrived in the outer office and wanted to discuss a possible case. Hungry but not wanting to see anyone turned away, Joe asked that the secretary send the man in.

"I was represented by a lawyer who moved to Portland before the case that he was handling for me could be brought to trial," the potential client began. "The reason this happened was that my lawsuit had been pending for about four years due to the courts being so jammed up. They couldn't get a trial date." "And you want me to take over?" Joe asked. The man nodded and said, "Yes."

Taking on the new client, Joe found it necessary to start over from scratch because he knew nothing of the case in question. A contractor, the client had a three-million-dollar contract with the city of Puyallup to build sewer lines. During the construction, he had incurred extra expenses due to the city changing some specifications while the work was in progress. Upon requesting compensation to cover the added

42-year-old Josef Diamond

expense of $250,000, he found that the city of Puyallup was loath to cough up anything above the amount specified by the original contract even though they had required the changes. Without the additional payment the client would suffer a substantial loss on the project. So, he sued to collect.

Looking into the matter, Joe learned that the lawyer representing the city of Puyallup was Archie Blair, a man he knew well and, in Joe's judgment, an honorable man. As the case was still pending, the statute of limitations did not apply, but it looked as though it could be another three years or so before the case finally came to trial. That was unacceptable because Joe's new client had already spent the extra money for the changes required by the city of Puyallup and was in need of a recovery without further delay.

Joe called Archie on the phone. "We ought to try to settle this case, Archie," Joe began. "I would love to do that," Archie agreed. "I have been trying to do that for a long time, but I don't know how it can be done." "Well," offered Joe, "I'll tell you what I'd like to do. Your client has not accepted the truth from my client. They have not believed in the merit of his position. So, I'd like to give you a real opportunity." "Go on," Archie answered, his interest was piqued.

"Since you represent the city of Puyallup," Joe proceeded to say, "I'm sure you can get permission to use the City Hall chambers as a courtroom, can't you?" "No problem" was Archie's response. "If you do that," Joe offered, "I will come down to your city hall with all of my witnesses and lay out my entire case before you without a judge being present. I will give you all of the facts that I have. I will put all of my witnesses on the stand, and you can cross-examine them as you wish." The unique offer continued, "You don't have to put on any testimony. You don't have to do anything if you don't want to."

Incredulous, Archie repeated, "I don't have to do anything?" "When we get through," proposed Joe, "if you think my case is worth $250,000, then I want a check for that amount. If you don't think it's worth that amount, we'll just forget the whole thing and we'll wait to go to trial whenever we can get a trial date, which will likely be two years or more down the road." "Yeah, at least," Archie acknowledged. "If we do this," Joe went on, "you will know everything about my case. You will be way ahead in preparing to litigate the case in court to protect your client."

"Let me see if I understand you correctly, Joe," queried Archie. "Are you saying that you will tell me everything your case is about? Hold back nothing? Offer all your facts and testimony, and I don't have to prepare anything or disclose anything to you?" "Uh-huh" was Joe's response. "And when you are finished, if I still believe my client is in the right you'll just wait until the matter goes to trial?" Archie continued to clarify what he had heard. "That's right," said Joe.

"It seems to me that I have everything to gain and nothing to lose. If I don't agree with your position, then I'll know what your case is all about and I'll know exactly how to defend my client," Archie noted with growing agreement in his tone of voice. "That's right," repeated Josef. "That sounds great to me," Archie said, "Let's do it!"

And so, Archie arranged to use the City Hall chambers, and Joe took all his witnesses down to Puyallup for two days of presentations, offering of documents, and testimony in support of his client's case. Archie cross-examined Joe's witnesses vigorously but did not put on any witnesses of his own.

At the end of the two days, Archie walked over to where Joe was seated and said, "Joe, you will get your check for $250,000." Joe accepted his offer and thanked him for his fairness.

Knowing that Archie was an honorable and fair man, Joe felt confident that, after listening to his case, Archie would see the wisdom of settling for the amount stipulated. Regrettably, Joe admits, "There are probably very few lawyers with whom something like this could be accomplished."

Joe and Archie settled the lawsuit saving everyone time, expense and frustration. And all of this without a judge being involved.

As readers must have determined by now, Joe was and is a gentle man. As Charles Carroll, once King County prosecutor, said, "I have actually seen him brush a mosquito off his arm rather than to swat and kill it."

Hal Harmon (not his real name) was soon to learn that as he entered Joe's office one sunny Tuesday (summer usually occurs on the third Tuesday in August between two o'clock and four o'clock in the afternoon in Seattle) to enlist his assistance in a personal legal problem.

"Have a seat, Mr. Harmon," Joe offered. "Tell me about your problem." "My father-in-law is in the process of losing his business," Harmon fretted. "He is a mechanical genius, trusting of everyone to a fault, and a very capable man, but he is no businessman. He allowed his son to run the business into the ground through accepting usurious loans and high living. Then he deserted his father and left him in a mess. When all of the facts came out, it put my father-in-law in the hospital and left me with the job of trying to salvage whatever could be salvaged."

With his mental wheels already turning, Joe nodded, and Hal continued his tale of woe. "The lenders have unscrupulously taken over operation of the company and are demanding that all of the stock be turned over to them. I want to sue and put them in jail. I want to do anything that would cause them as much grief as they have caused my father-in-law."

"You can sue and maybe win," Joe said, beginning to present his thoughts, "but if you're just out to hurt someone, you'll have to find yourself another lawyer." It didn't take Hal long to accept Joe's counsel. He asked Joe to pursue the case. The results reflected the wisdom of Joe's approach. Winning the case, Joe received 20 times the book value of the company for Hal's troubled father-in-law.

"I would never want to get into any legal battle with anyone but you in my corner," Hal later complimented Joe. "On the other hand, if we wound up on opposite sides, neither would I be afraid."

MEMORIES

"Years ago, I remember well in my mind, Josef was in front of his house on Lake Washington—Joe was between 40 and 50 years old—trying to water ski. Joe had two skis on and had a big cigar in his mouth. He was all set to take off. Then he started to take off—the boat went faster and faster, and Joe sank deeper and deeper until all you could see was his head sticking up and the cigar still sticking out of his mouth.

"It was one of the funniest sights I have ever seen. Each time I think of it I still get a good laugh."

– Leon Diamond
Joe's younger brother and
partner in Diamond Parking

From Richard C. Evans, president and CEO, West One Bank, Bellevue, came this accolade: "Josef wrote the book on negotiating! I have left his office wringing wet after tough and lengthy discussions and negotiations only to have him look up from his desk on my way out, smile and say, 'Dick, I really enjoyed talking with you today.' So, instead of feeling like you just finished Negotiations 101, Josef has a way of making you feel good, and still do the transactions.

"I have noticed that Josef cares a great deal for people. When he was selling one of his companies, his first and lasting concern was for the employees of the company and that they were cared for and treated fairly.

"In my 35 years of banking, I cannot think of a more interesting client relationship. If he likes you and trusts you, he sends you referral busi-

ness, and his business. He is demanding and expects performance. However, he provides the same in return. He is extremely loyal. It is a privilege to know Josef, and I greatly honor his friendship."

Harley Hoppe said, "When I was county assessor, Joe came in one day and complained about his property taxes being too high and that we should do something about them. When asked if he would sell any of his properties for the assessed value, he said, 'Of course not, the properties are worth more than that.' I, therefore, wasn't able to be of much help."

CHAPTER ELEVEN
SUING HIS OWN CLIENT

The voice on the other end of the phone pleaded, "Joe, you have to come down here. I've got real problems." The voice was that of a man we'll call Paul Herman. Paul was a grubbing contractor whose service is to remove trees and stumps.

"You've got to come to Portland, Joe," Paul continued. "This is short notice I know, but I'm in trouble." Not only was it short notice, it was three days before Christmas, which in itself wasn't of great significance to Joe, but three days' notice requires some substantial shuffling of appointments and other obligations to attend holiday functions given by his friends.

"What's the problem, Paul?" Joe inquired. As Paul's problems were laid out it became evident that the government had given the logs in a soon-to-be-flooded area to Portland General Electric, but stump removal was Paul's responsibility, and due to certain government requirements, his contract with PGE was affected. Consequently, Paul was going to lose a great deal of money on his million-dollar contract. The matter closely paralleled one that Joe had handled for a contractor friend who had sued the city of Puyallup.

"I lost a lot of money on this job, Joe, and PGE won't pay for my extras. I think I have a good claim, but I need to have it settled before year end because of income tax problems." Joe knew that going up against a major power company was difficult at best, but to try to effect a settlement in a matter of days against such a behemoth could be next to impossible. But like many people who called Joe for legal assistance, Paul was a friend. Joe agreed to travel to Portland to see what could be done to help his friend.

Joe hadn't discussed a fee with Paul the previous day, but then, he never inquired of a client as to their ability to pay for his services. His criterion for taking on a client had always been based on the merits of the case. Whether the client's claim was justified was his first consideration always. Money, in his mind, was secondary. Those who know Joe Diamond know that this is true.

After the four-hour drive in wintry weather (fortunately, no snow to contend with), Joe reviewed the documents and related material with his client and then paid a visit to the house counsel for Portland General Electric. He laid out his client's claim for what he felt were valid extras over and above the original contract. He informed the house counsel that his client was seeking a reasonable award of $250,000. "Absolutely not," blustered the PGE lawyer. "This is a lump sum contract. We're not going to pay any more than the contract calls for." "Well," offered Joe, "you leave me no alternative. I guess we're going to have to sue."

Borrowing an office that evening from a lawyer friend, and working most of the night, Joe prepared a complaint against the power giant for nearly a million dollars. He included everything he could reasonably include in the complaint. The fact that the government wasn't being treated fairly because it was giving away more timber than it realized was some of the language used. The point that PGE was provided a windfall benefit from the sale of the timber became part of the complaint as well as the extra time and effort expended by Joe and his client being sufficient cause for some of the extra compensation. Some of the elements of the complaint would not necessarily be included under normal circumstances and would, in fact, normally be saved for court testimony, but Joe was anxious to resolve the matter quickly for the sake of his client.

Appearing in the opposing counsel's office the next morning, tired after getting very little sleep while preparing the complaint, Joe informed him, "I just came back to let you know that I am starting this lawsuit. I don't know whether or not you want to accept service, but if you will, it will save me having a process server perform service on PGE."

The seemingly indifferent lawyer accepted service of the complaint and asked, "All right. Now, what do you want me to do about it?" "I'd simply like you to take the time to read it," responded Joe. "Maybe you'll have second thoughts about the possibility of settling the matter."

With a look that clearly showed his contempt for the intrusion on his valuable time, the PGE attorney began to read as Joe sat across the desk from him. As he continued to read, Joe noted a marked change in his demeanor. By the time the PGE attorney had read the six-page document, his look had changed to one of resignation. Without a word he opened his center drawer, took out the firm's checkbook, and wrote a check for $250,000.

Paul was greatly pleased with the result of Joe's efforts as he gladly accepted the check, which Joe had signed over to him. It was the night before Christmas and all through his office … Paul had become a believer in Santa Claus in the person of Joe Diamond.

One might think this is the end of the story, but in reality it is only the end of the beginning of the tale. There was a matter of payment for services yet to be handled.

Back in his office, Joe thought about it some and decided that a billing for 10 percent of the recovery, substantially less than the usual contingency fee, would be an adequate amount for his services. He caused a billing to be sent to Paul for $25,000.

Two days later, his friend was on the phone. "Joe, I just got your bill in the mail," he protested, "and I have to tell you that

I'm not going to pay you any $25,000 for the day-and-a-half you spent on the matter. It just isn't worth it!"

Always willing to negotiate, Joe responded, "I thought 10 percent was a fair amount, considering the recovery, Paul, but I'm willing to discuss it with you." He continued, "Tell me what you think is fair. Do you want to cut it in half? I'd be willing to settle on that basis."

"No way!" the belligerent client blurted. "I'm not going to pay you any $12,000! I'm not even going to pay you ten thousand!" Taking a deep breath and counting to 10, mostly because he disliked these kinds of conversations, Joe asked, "What are you willing you pay, Paul?" "I won't pay you a nickel over eleven hundred." Paul blurted, "One thousand one hundred dollars for the time you put in!"

"Well, Paul," Joe answered in a matter-of-fact tone, "As a matter of principle, I can't settle for that. I'm sorry to do this but you leave me no choice. I'm going to have to sue you for payment." "See you in court!" Paul curtly replied, followed by a louder than usual click and a dial tone.

Joe asked a lawyer friend to represent him. Paul wasn't quite as successful in finding a Seattle attorney to take his case because many Seattle lawyers knew and liked Joe, and moreover, it's a little difficult to find a lawyer to represent someone who isn't willing to pay his lawyer.

Finally, Paul settled on a Portland attorney to represent him. Their first move was to insist upon a jury trial, probably with the thought that a jury might not hold lawyers in very high esteem and would balk at awarding such a large sum of money for a day and a half of work. Upon hearing this, Joe pretty much concluded that he could be in a little bit of trouble. Claiming $25,000 in front of a jury might prove disastrous. He decided his chances of collecting the full amount was remote, but he felt confident that he'd collect more than the offered $1,100.

The gavel fell and the trial began.

As the only witness for the plaintiff, Joe testified that the amount he was requesting was a more than fair fee for the recovery won. The defendant's lawyer argued that Joe be paid only the small sum that Paul had already offered.

The jury was out only an hour. Joe, his lawyer, and Paul, along with his attorney, were called back into the courtroom. The jury was coming in.

The foreman asked a question: "Is the jury limited to allowing $25,000 asked for by the plaintiff? Are we allowed to award more?" The faces of Paul and his lawyer sagged and blanched. "You cannot award more than the plaintiff has sued for," the judge responded. Once again, the jury repaired to the jury room.

After only a few minutes, the jury returned and found for Joe. "We find for the plaintiff the sum of $25,000."

As you might imagine, there was an appeal but it went for naught. Joe eventually collected the fee that in his mind was exceedingly fair.

As an interesting side note, Paul's then teenage son went on to law school, passed the bar, and became a lawyer.

MEMORIES

"I was a deputy prosecutor in the office of a good friend of Joe's, Charles O. Carroll, who for many years was the prosecuting attorney for King County. At the time, I was also program chairman for a large political club in Seattle. This was in the early 1950s, when a hot debate was raging over where the I-5 freeway should be located. Joe had almost single-handedly taken on the powerful highway establishment and spoke out publicly against the concept of a 'big ditch' through the middle of downtown Seattle. He consented to speak to my club. It was a real 'stem-winder' of a speech and impressed me sufficiently that, when I left the prosecutor's office for private practice, it was to go with his law firm (Lycette, Diamond & Sylvester), where I spent several years as an associate.

"I hadn't been in Joe's office long before it became crystal clear that this was 'some lawyer!' I firmly believe to this day—not only is Josef Diamond one of the most successful businessmen I have ever met, but he is also on the best lawyers that I have ever met. The uniqueness of

this is that he is the only person I have ever known who is absolutely top flight in both the legal profession and the world of business. A remarkable man is my friend Joe Diamond.

– James A. Anderson
Justice, Supreme Court of the state of Washington

"I remember El Salvador about 35 years ago. Joe's client was in the foul prison in the center of San Salvador, and Joe was trying to get him out. The client was the contractor on a stretch of the Pan American Highway; he was a Seattle sewer contractor who thought he had 'fixed' his contract. When he ran out of money, his fixer disappeared and he tried to drive across the Guatemalan border—without success.

"I represented the sureties on his bond—I had all the money. So I was wined and dined by the local bankers, the minister of public works, etc. Joe, on the other hand, was sure they were going to throw him into prison along with his client. He urged me to pay the government the bond proceeds so he and his client could go home. I wanted indemnity for my poor insurers, of course, so Joe and I got pretty well acquainted over a couple of weeks. Joe's client was willing to sign anything to get out of that awful jail. Eventually my Canadian sureties paid 100 percent and we all went home.

– John Ehrlichman

CHAPTER TWELVE
DIAMOND PARKING GROWS

The early growth of Diamond Parking was nothing short of phenomenal during the 1950s. With younger brother, Leon, the operating partner, working closely with Josef, new Diamond Parking locations began to pop up on what might have appeared to the casual observer to be every other block all over Seattle.

It was about this time, 1951, when Josef's son, 14-year-old Joel, began getting involved in the family business. Much like his father before him, he spent his time pumping gas and cleaning windshields, along with pulling weeds and general upkeep of, among others, a parking lot and service station the company had at 2010 Western—"Old Number One" (the location no longer exists)—while going to school and later on to college.

Diamond Parking headquarters was located at 1318 Madison in the basement of the Seattle Medical Center, which was one of the properties developed by Joe's older brother, Louis, in the 1940s. The company remained there for many years and thrived while it grew. With the very able assistance of Mike Gemza, Mert Sweeting, and, of course, the ubiquitous Gene Detroit, the in-house general contractor, Leon Diamond was in daily operational control while his and Joe's sister Jean Howse was in charge of the office. Let me say that again. She was in charge of the office!

Jean Howse ran the office activities with an iron hand, and the results indicate she did a respectable job of it. There were, however, a few little procedures that slowed things down. For example, at one time Jean proclaimed that no mail would be opened in that office by anyone other than herself. It is reasonable to assume that she looked at it as a security measure, considering the cash and check payments that might arrive by mail. The problem was that since no mail could be opened unless she opened it, nothing much got done before Jean arrived at the office each morning, and she definitely was not a willing early riser.

A block away from this basement headquarters was a McDonald's fast-food restaurant. On Saturdays, when Joe could always be found at the parking office (at least in the early hours before he made his rounds to check the condition of the company's many properties), McDonald's was the lunch venue of choice. Joe loved ketchup (or catsup—whichever you prefer) and added it in large quantities to his hamburger and french fries. Considering his great love of this condiment, I once commented to him, "Joe, I think you'd put ketchup on

Joe Diamond says hi to Dan MacMillan, a UW marketing student who works part time chalking overtime cars near Occidental Park.

ice cream." He looked at me, kind of puzzled, and said, "And what's wrong with that?"

Diamond Parking remained a Seattle-only operation for many years. Joe wanted it that way. He had no wish to expand beyond Seattle and made that very clear to everyone in the organization. Then came the day in the midsixties when a man who owned a department store in downtown Aberdeen, Washington, turned his business over to his son. Because he wanted the store to have its own parking lot on the adjacent piece of property, which he also owned, he went to his bankers at the nearby National Bank of Commerce and asked if they had any suggestions about creating and running a parking lot.

National Bank of Commerce (later to become Rainier Bank, then Security Pacific Bank, then Seafirst Bank, and most recently Bank of America) was also Diamond Parking's banker in Seattle. They quickly recommended Diamond Parking to their Aberdeen customer. The contact was made, and a process that Joe was decidedly against began to take form.

Soon after the initial contact, Joe, Leon, son Joel, who was getting more and more involved in the management level of the business, and Gene Detroit made the drive to Aberdeen to look over the property. Everyone knew how Joe felt about parking locations remote from Seattle, so they weren't surprised when, upon looking over the property, Joe said he was not interested. Similarly, Leon said he wanted nothing to do with running an operation away from closely supervised Seattle. After listening a few minutes, Detroit spoke up and said, "If you guys don't want it, I'll take it on." "I'll run it for Diamond Parking," Joel quickly interjected. Not wishing to be a stumbling block for his son, who was just beginning to flex his wings, Joe acquiesced.

Thus the first out-of-Seattle location was born for Diamond Parking. Joel, over what had been the stated objections of Joe and Leon, opened that location and hired a retired Boston policeman to look after the operation—keep it looking clean and respectably well kept as well as picking up the money from the slotted cash box. An avid golfer, the man only worked two days one week and three days the next, squeezed in between tee times. Even so the operation did reasonably well.

Things just naturally happened after that. Even though Joe was against expansion outside of Seattle and Leon was pretty much retired, Joel proceeded to open locations with the help of real estate negotiator Jim Roberts in such places as Tacoma, Yakima, Wenatchee, and Spokane. Joel had little interest in the Seattle operations. His goal was expansion into other cities and other states. Soon Diamond Parking operations began to surface in Idaho, Utah, and elsewhere. Josef was becoming enamored with the expansion that his son was bringing about. Joel was fully involved in these new locations, and though Leon made it known he wanted to retire for health reasons, he declined from taking over the Seattle operations.

After much back-and-forth discussion, there came a gathering of many Diamond family friends and associates at Canlis' Restaurant in Seattle to announce that Joel Diamond was going to take over the entire operation as president and CEO.

There's more to Joe Diamond than parking

The Associated Press

SEATTLE — Joe Diamond's image with the motoring public isn't exactly polished, but they know him: He's the guy who makes them pay for parking in numerous lots throughout the Northwest and Alaska.

"They're all afraid of him. They think he's a zillionaire," says Harry Kessler.

A longtime friend, Kessler calls Diamond "a teddy bear."

His record as a lawyer, however, suggests more of a tiger. His legal work set the stage for a landmark Supreme Court ruling on minority quotas for graduate school admission.

Diamond, former president of the National Parking Association, says he doesn't let his public image bother him, even if he thinks it's wrong.

"Everybody thinks I'm just in it for the money. I'm not," he says.

"I've got a tough skin," he adds. "I live with myself."

Diamond Parking, one of the city's oldest continually operated businesses, was started 65 years ago by Louis Diamond, an older brother.

Joe Diamond, one of two brothers who were handed the business by Louis in 1946, says he doesn't know of an older parking company anywhere.

A son of Russian immigrants, Diamond says he is worth "many millions." He doesn't know exactly, he says, but in a 1979 court document he estimated he and his wife were worth $13.5 million.

He has invested in real estate, construction, shopping malls, a silver mine, banking and oil explorations and is a director of 30 corporations.

Joe Diamond, known primarily for his parking lots, is also a successful lawyer and businessman.
(Credit: *Anchorage Daily News*, Saturday, August 10, 1985)

Joe became chairman of the board of directors. It was quite a party that night at the beautiful restaurant overlooking Lake Union with several people becoming a little happier than under ordinary circumstances. Johnny Cain (Joe's partner in Budget Rent A Car) and Joel managed do some serious damage to a bottle of Napoleon brandy. The party was a success.

Offices in other states continued to be opened; Oregon, California, Hawaii, and Alaska were added to the list. Then, along came Arizona, Utah, and Montana, not necessarily in that order. Diamond Parking also began operating in another country—Vancouver, B.C., Canada.

Currently, Diamond Parking, the largest and oldest family-owned parking operation in the world, operates over a thousand parking lots and garages in nine states. In addition to these many parking locations, other commercial properties have been acquired in a number of different cities and states. The Paulsen Building in Spokane (the second largest in that Washington city) is one the properties owned by this empire.

Joel and his wife, Julie, have two grown children, Jonathon and Cindy. Jonathon took over as president of Diamond Parking after he graduated from the University of Washington and finished his master's degree at Duke University. The company is continuing to thrive under his capable direction and with input from both his father, Joel, and his grandfather Josef. The future continues to look bright for Diamond Parking.

MEMORIES

"When we think about Joe Diamond we think about our grandfather, whom we have always called Gumpa. Growing up, we remember our grandfather best through our Sunday visits to his home in Laurelhurst, where, together with our cousins Michelle and Steven we swam in the indoor pool and had lunch and special times with our grandparents.

"Another of our fondest memories is on holidays such as Christmas when our grandmother and grandfather would restructure their home so the grandchildren got full run of the downstairs portion of the house.

"These are just a few of the special moments that we remember and will always hold very dear to our hearts.

"As we have grown up through the years, our grandfather has always been an extraordinary part of our lives. He has always been there for us in every possible way, supported us in all our decisions. Even though neither of us relived his dream of going to law school, we feel that he is supportive and proud of our decisions of education and what we have decided to do in our lives."

– Cindy and Jonathon Diamond

"We first became acquainted approximately 25 years ago when I took over the parking industry jurisdiction for the Teamsters Union. At the time, some of our mutual friends had passed the word around that I had stated I was going to straighten out Diamond Parking, which was not true, and that Josef Diamond would never negotiate a contract with Jim Clark. Well, we let this ride for some time, Josef being as stubborn as he is and I being a bit bullheaded. Finally, however, I called Josef and we talked, straightened out what we had both said and hadn't said, negotiated a fine contract, and have been close friends ever since.

"Another little story about Josef. My secretaries used to complain that Josef was rude on the telephone. Now, I know Josef might be a little bit stubborn, bullheaded, and tough, but never rude, so I asked my secretaries why they felt this way about Josef. They said when Josef called the office and I was not in, he would simply say something to the effect, 'Have him call Joe Diamond,' and hang up, never saying good-bye or anything else. I told Josef about this and he felt bad, but in his usual manner he said, 'I just haven't anything else to say and we're all busy.'

"In closing I would like to say Josef Diamond is one of the warmest, toughest, most decent men I have ever known, and I am very happy to be counted among his friends.

– E. J. "Jim" Clark

"The 'One and Only' Joe Diamond is my father.

"He is very special to me and my family not only because he built an empire that will continue to provide for us for many years to come, but because he is a very warm and loving person. He has been a role model for me and just about every other person that he has come into contact with.

"I have learned a great deal from my father throughout my life and continue to learn each and every day. His wisdom, intelligence, love, and kindness are his most outstanding attributes. His dogged determination to get a problem resolved is unceasing. He sees all projects through to the finish no matter how many obstacles are in his way.

"I love my father very much and am proud to be his son."

– Joel Diamond

"I met Mr. Diamond in about 1958 when I first started working on the maintenance staff for his parking lots. I drew my first opinion of him as an old crab. As I got to know him better, I changed my thinking. I think he is a wonderful person and very concerned about his devoted employees.

"In later years I became in charge of maintenance and construction of the parking end of the business. At one time I was building a parking

lot when Mr. Diamond drove by. He later called me on the phone and wanted to know whose car was there with a 'saddle on the back.' (It was a Porsche with an air spoiler on the back.) I told him it was a contractor's car. His reply, 'If he can afford a car like that you're paying him too much.'

"One other time he called and chewed on me. I tried to get a word in. Finally I got mad at him and told him he had the mouth of an alligator and the heart of a lamb. He said that was a pretty good description. I did not know what he was talking about and said so. But that didn't stop him. He started on me again. Why? I don't know, it was my job to find out."

– Frank Carter

CHAPTER THIRTEEN
CAR RENTAL LIFE BEGINS

With Diamond Parking growing in leaps and bounds, Joe was always on the lookout for additional properties suited for high-volume parking locations. He became aware of such a property on the corner of 8th Avenue and Pike Street in Seattle. It was an old, one-story building with several small shops as tenants, among which were a Chinese laundry, a shoe repair shop, and a small, local car rental company being operated by the property owner, Dave Litvin.

Since Litvin for many years had operated a parking and car rental operation called Windsor Garage and U-Drive in the old Windsor parking garage adjoining the Windsor Hotel on 6th Avenue and Union Street in downtown Seattle, Joe knew him through the National Parking Association. When the old, wooden Windsor Garage was demolished to make way for a modern parking facility, Dave Litvin had moved his car rental operation to the property he owned at 8th and Pike and reverted to the original name (from 1928), Seattle U-Drive.

With two full-time employees (the writer being one of them) and a part-timer, Dave was enjoying life. He wasn't working very hard because the small company returned a reasonable profit with very little effort—at least from the owner's standpoint. Dave showed up every morning about 10 o'clock or a little later, had a look in the cash drawer, offered a mumbled curse, and left to spend a large portion of his day at Walston and Company, a local stock brokerage with a running report on the "big board" at Wall Street in New York. Seemingly, his only complaint in life at that point was his frequently mentioned failing health. He often talked of a weak heart, and in fact, several years later, he did have a pacemaker installed. He dreamed of enjoying his not insignificant personal fortune in the balmy breezes of Hawaii with his wife of many years, Jennie.

At one of the parking association meetings, Joe approached Litvin to inquire whether he had any thoughts of selling his property at a fair price so that it could be demolished for use as a parking lot. What he may not have known at the time was that Dave Litvin was anxious to convert his property and car rental company into the additional nest egg that would allow him to retire and live a life of luxury. It wasn't long afterward that he and Joe were in serious conversation about the sale.

Dave had a stipulation, however, that Joe wasn't willing to consider. He wanted to sell not only his property but also his U-Drive company, and the price for the U-Drive alone would be $50,000. Joe declined. He simply wasn't interested in owning a car rental business of which he knew nothing and of which he had heard some tales of less-than-honorable dealings.

Litvin began to actively seek someone willing to take on the U-Drive company. He thought of another acquaintance from the parking association—John Cain, who owned a highly successful Shell service station only a couple of blocks away on the corner 9th and Olive next to the Camlin Hotel.

Litvin approached John Cain (affectionately known as Johnny by almost everyone) with the proposal and had his immediate attention. Johnny Cain was an entrepreneur in the strictest sense of the word. He, like Joe Diamond, was always looking for new challenges. He quickly agreed to making whatever arrangement could be worked out to take over Seattle U-Drive as a 50/50 partner with Joe, whom he also knew. There was only one problem, he didn't have the money to swing his half of the deal.

Dave approached Joe with the proposal, and though reluctant, Joe got together with Dave and Johnny to buy the U-Drive company, in addition to the property, which was what he wanted to begin with. He agreed that the present tenants could remain until their leases ran out.

Joe advanced the amount Johnny couldn't come up with to buy his half of Seattle U-Drive with the understanding that Cain would pay him back out of future profits. John Cain agreed. Joe now owned half of a car rental company that he didn't really want. As a matter of fact, he didn't even want his name associated with the company until he could be sure that it was being operated honestly and with respect for its customers.

So it was that in 1961 Johnny Cain showed up one day and began to haggle with Dave over the purchase of certain furniture and fixtures. The conversation went something like this, "I'll give you $50 for the rolltop desk, $25 for the chair, and another $25 for the guy sitting in it." That was me. That's the first time we, the employees of Seattle U-Drive, knew that a deal had been struck and that we now worked for Joe Diamond and John Cain.

I won't dwell on me very much because I'm not what this story is about. But I will mention that I was suspicious of Joe Diamond because of all of the derogatory things I'd heard about him from people who didn't know anything about him. Moreover, I was highly suspicious of Johnny Cain—not because of derogatory comments but because he had two or three longtime, loyal employees at his service station and I figured that as soon as he knew how to operate a car rental company, he would dispose of me, Sammy (Burnett Sams), and part-timer Hank (Henry Ader) in favor of his old employees.

Because of these suspicions and the fact that I had a family to support, I decided to take the test to become a policeman in Lynnwood, 15 miles north of Seattle and nearer to my home. It happens that I scored, much to my surprise, second from the top. The top scorer had some physical problem, such as a toe growing out of the middle of his forehead or something, that left me as the top candidate.

After working days and riding many nights with Chief Glandt's officers at the chief's request, it came down to one day before I was to be sworn in. From a reserve officer who had decided to discontinue his association with the Lynnwood Police Department, I had already purchased a handsome leather utility belt including a sap (yes, police carried a sap in those days) and holster, uniforms, and a .38 police special revolver. Since I had given Johnny Cain notice well in advance, he approached me on the final day and asked if I would consider staying on and becoming a manager of his Seattle U-Drive company. It was a sucker offer because it ended up with me working longer with no increase in pay, but I was young and I jumped at it. "A manager!" I thought. "If only my high school classmates could see me now." I called Chief Glandt with my regrets and became a manager in name, though not in fact. I was still the head car washer. I will end this little story about me with the thought that I shall forever be grateful to the late Johnny Cain and his partner, Josef Diamond, for their guidance. When our little company, which was to become Budget Rent A Car of Washington-Oregon, Inc., was sold to the home corporation years later, I had gone from navy bomb loader extraordinaire (other swabbies called us BB stackers) to car washer without a high school education to executive vice president and general manager of a multi-million dollar corporation.

Okay. Enough of that. Let's get back to Joe Diamond and Seattle U-Drive. As Seattle U-Drive proved itself to Joe as being honorable and above board, he became more and more interested in its operation. I'm sure he saw it as a great challenge. While the employees didn't see much of him, he did have many meetings with Cain and dropped by fairly often on a Saturday to see how we were doing and to look over the operation and, as was his habit in his parking locations, to look for weeds that needed to be pulled.

Here I should offer another aside. Our little Seattle U-Drive company with its 28 cars, many of them two or three years old, was a tough operation to manage. We survived primarily on the car rental needs of insurance company claimants, who, by the way, are some of the toughest customers in the business because they feel everything is owed them. Another significant but difficult source of business was the castoffs from Hertz, located five or six blocks away. If Hertz didn't feel comfortable that the customer was fully responsible, they referred him or her to us. I must say we became quite proficient at dealing with marginally qualified car renters. Part of our business also was derived from the infamous "roofing and siding" salesmen. They were, for the most part, crookeder than a dog's hind leg. When it came time to pay the bill, these guys could disappear with a "poof" that would have made Houdini jealous.

Many was the rainy night that I spent hiding in the bushes, waiting for some freeloader, who had no intention of paying for his rental, to return home so I could repossess (usually covertly with the spare keys as I'm not big enough to confront most people) our long-overdue vehicle.

It was 1961 and the World's Fair was almost upon us. We began slowly to build our fleet, thanks to Joe's almost unlimited credit at what was then called the National Bank of Commerce. Just as the World's Fair opened its gate, we reached a peak of 68 cars, most of them reasonably new and all of them carefully maintained.

In the meantime, a few blocks away, an upstart car rental company called Budget Rent A Car began an operation on the triangular corner where Westlake Avenue and Virginia Street dissected 7th Avenue. At the time, the entire industry was renting its full-size cars at $10 a day and 10 cents a mile including gas when along came this interloper (directly across the street from National Car Rental, I might add) with a massive, rotating sign on a tall pole above its tiny rental office building proclaiming for all the world to see as they drove by—$5 a day and 5 cents a mile! It was almost a toss-up as to which was larger, the rotating sign or the diminutive rental office.

Some of us snickered at this ridiculous entry into the car rental field but not Joe. He was beginning to grasp the complexity of the car rental business, and he knew that in order for us to grow we needed to have an affiliation with a family of offices around the country so that our cars could be reserved in advance of a traveler arriving in our city.

As the World's Fair continued, Seattle U-Drive was doing well. Our cars were booked solid, and Johnny Cain even rented his own 1954 Chevrolet station wagon. When cars are in short supply, a customer will settle for just about anything and be happy to get it. The income from those rentals of his personal car went into the company, not to Johnny; he was ultimately fair to the company.

Near the end of the World's Fair, Joe and Johnny approached the owners of that little Budget Rent A Car franchise and soon learned that they had lost money during the fair. Their $50,000 investment had shrunk to $45,000. They were anxious to sell; both of them were fully involved in other business interests and ready to unload their unsuccessful venture.

Now it became Joe's task to persuade Budget Rent A Car Corporation, whose president and cofounder was Jules Lederer (then husband of Ann Landers). Jules, in an effort to increase his Budget Rent A Car representation around the country, had sidled up to the National Parking Association, of which Joe was the president at the time. He wanted Joe to persuade other large parking entities to take on Budget franchises, which he guessed (correctly as it turns out) would work well in conjunction with parking facilities.

Joe told Jules that he had a tentative agreement with the Seattle Budget operators to take over their franchise, but Jules balked because Joe already was operating Seattle U-Drive and was unwilling to give it up as Jules was insisting he do. Further, he thought Johnny Cain was too old. Jules was looking for young, hungry people who would be willing to work long and hard hours toward success. Johnny Cain may not have been young (kinda depends on your own age/vantage point, doesn't it?), but in all other respects, he was exactly what Jules was looking for even if Jules didn't know it at the time.

Soooo .... Joe got Jules drunk (which wasn't very hard to do in those days) and not only sold him on Johnny Cain but got him to agree to let us keep Seattle U-Drive operating out of the same office as Budget and, further, to forgive for all time franchise fees on the 68 cars we brought to the franchise. The dollars saved over the 38 years we had the franchise was impressive.

We became Budget Rent A Car of Washington early in 1963. As Johnny and Joe were looking over the furniture, fixtures, and fleet in order to make an offer, Johnny said to the operating partner of the previous ownership, "Pat, the tires are all bald!" Pat responded, "So what? They're round, ain't they?" I knew then that he was from the "old school," the one in which I had cut my teeth.

With the purchase of Budget, in addition to our well-maintained Seattle U-Drive fleet, we added some real tired Corvairs, Falcons, Fairlane 500s, and Chevrolet Impalas—all with bald tires. We were now Budget Rent A Car with our large $5 a day and 5 cents a mile sign spinning around and swaying in the breeze above our office. We changed all the tires and began our long journey with Budget Rent A Car.

50 The Seattle Times   Wednesday, July 20, 1966

John J. Reddin's

Faces of the City

'The Smartest Guy I Know'

JOHN CAIN

Josef Diamond, left, played host at a picnic for his employes and friends. He chatted with Leonard Decker, center, picnic chairman, and brother, Leon Diamond.

MEMORIES

"I remember how I met him," wrote Jim Daly, then vice president of Rainier Bank (previously National Bank of Commerce). *"Joe had just purchased the Budget Rent A Car franchise in partnership with John Cain, who was also in the parking business, operating a lot adjacent to the Camlin Hotel on Olive Way.*

"And that reminds me of my favorite story about Josef that I was part of: It was Friday afternoon, the start of a three-day Memorial Day

weekend. Downtown Seattle was pretty well shut down. I tried phoning his law office in the Hoge Building—switchboard was down. The bank needed to get together with Joe. At 4:30, I went down to the deserted law offices, saw a light down at the end and found Joe hard at work. I wasn't too surprised.

"One evening, my wife, Sally, and I accompanied Joe and Vi to a planned dinner engagement. We parked the car on a Diamond Parking lot and started on our way to the restaurant. Deep in conversation, we suddenly noticed the absence of Joe as we walked. Retracing our steps, we found our friend Joe pulling grass and weeds that had grown up in the cracks of the cement on the Diamond lot. We waited for our gardener to finish his chores and continued on our way without missing a beat. That's Joe!!"

"During the ten years [I've known him] I have spoken to Joe from time to time on the phone, but our escrow closings all were by delivery, instructions by delivery, and telephone, all quite successful, and I never spent any time with him in person until one day in January of this year [1990] when he bought my lunch for me.

"The legend became a reality, and I can't tell you how much I enjoyed that short time together, to get to know more about him personally. It comes as no surprise: He is a gracious, gentle giant, an accomplished and successful attorney, an astute businessman, and a true gentleman. He comes from the old school of honesty when a handshake would bind an agreement to be respected years later. In my years (and growing) of meeting wealthy and so-called worldly business clients in our community, I've learned that the only people who don't

like fellows like Joe are those who are dishonest and envy the success of an honest man.

"Josef Diamond has always portrayed strength and position with humility."

– Ruth A. Houghton
Transamerica Insurance Company

"A funny story I recall is when Joe and a friend were going somewhere in his friend's Volvo. As they moved through the city they saw many Budget trucks traveling around on rental. The way I understand the story, they had pulled in behind one of those rented Budget trucks at a stoplight [on one of Seattle's steep hills], and Joe was telling his friend all about the Budget truck fleet. I would have given anything to have been there at that moment when the Budget truck proceeded to back onto the hood of his friend's Volvo. I don't know if this is exactly how it happened, but for several weeks after, at our Saturday morning meetings, Joe wanted to know who was renting those hundred trucks and did we check to see if the renters knew how to drive at all.

"Joe made working a pleasure for me and I miss those days at Budget very much."

– Dave Jones
Then Manager of
Budget's truck rental division

CHAPTER FOURTEEN
GOV-MART IS BORN

Discount warehouse stores such as Costco are everywhere today, but that wasn't the case in the mid-20th century. There may have been "big box" stores in California, but there were certainly none in the Pacific Northwest. It was in the mid-1950s that Joe was contacted by two men from California who had been referred to him by an old army acquaintance from Fort Lewis. One of the men was the owner of a savings bank, and the other was the operator of a discount merchandise store where only members were permitted to shop.

These two partners wanted to open a similar discount store in the Seattle area and wanted Joe to represent them in legal matters. Searching Seattle for a suitable large building, the trio settled on an old, very well-known but now closed dance hall, the Trianon Ballroom at Third Avenue and Wall Street, just a few blocks from the core of Seattle.

As the members-only discount store was set up, Joe's thoughts that he would only represent the company as its lawyer were soon displaced with other ideas proffered by the two partners. "The only way you can act as our lawyer, Joe, is if you own part of the corporation," they informed him. "That's the way we like to operate. Either you become a part owner, or we'll have to find someone else to represent us legally."

Though it was against his principles to have an interest in a business of a client, Joe finally agreed to take a 15 percent interest in the venture. He later opined, "It's one of the more exciting business ventures ever for me." At heart, Joe was a retailer.

Starting off as Fed-Mart, the outlet gave the impression that it was available only to government employees who would pay $5.00 to join and $1.50 a year thereafter to maintain the membership. The reality was that just about everyone was acceptable as a member since just about everyone had some remote or past relationship with the government, such as military service. The name Fed-Mart was changed when the California owners of a store of the same name complained, and Gov-Mart came into being. The operation was almost an instant success. Only a short time went by before Gov-Mart had enrolled over 250,000 members and earned an overwhelming $1.25 million dollars in membership fees alone.

In the 18,000-square-foot facility, the very first year's gross earnings were in excess of $12,000,000. Initially, the pricing strategy for both stores was to mark a price on an item and add, in large, bold letters "PLUS 10%." The buyer's impression might be that the item was being sold at 10% above cost, which was not necessarily the case, nor would Josef have agreed to that pricing strategy if it was intended to mislead. The Federal Trade Commission, in a formal complaint, viewed this practice as being deceptive. An immediate change was made so that each item was marked at its actual selling price.

Despite the change in the pricing strategy, the Feds stepped in and charges were filed against Gov-Mart requiring the collection of "damages" incurred during the "plus 10%" pricing era. In from Washington, D.C., a battery of Federal Trade Commission employees spent an initial four days in hearings involving the store. Thereafter they bounced back and forth between D.C. and Seattle like yo-yos for a time. The FTC hearings proved to be a long, arduous process for Joe, but Gov-Mart customers were loyal to a fault and continued to support their local discount store.

Seattle was so supportive that a very large cardboard thermometer was constructed close to the Gov-Mart store by dedicated well-wishers, for everyone to see. The thermometer reflected the most recent activities of the Federal Trade Commission hearings. Made of colored construction paper, the thermometer would escalate to "GREAT" on a day when Gov-Mart fared well in the hearings. On bad days for the operation, the thermometer would show a precipitous drop to sub-zero temperatures with a sad note attached.

After a while, the FTC dismissed their action against Gov-Mart, packed their bags and returned to Washington, D.C. Gov-Mart and its supporters had won a decisive victory.

It was in 1959 that Jerry Alhadeff became manager of the store. He had been hired as a trainee to be assistant manager of a planned South Tacoma Gov-Mart facility, but due to the departure of the then manager, Jerry (with a long history in his family's seafood business but nothing in retail), because of his obvious abilities, was elevated the manager position.

With no more interference from the government, the outlet in South Tacoma was opened to great local fanfare. The South Tacoma store, like the one in Seattle, was an overnight success and began to gross millions. Despite these successes, however, Joe's partners, who may have had some concern over Seattle's reputation for rain, approached him and asked him to buy the entire business. They wanted to move back to San Diego. Having no aversion to owning a thriving business and with minimum trepidation because of his faith in Alhadeff's inherent management capabilities, Joe bought out the two. With the two gone, Joe sought another partner. Eventually, Alex Shulman became that partner. They formed Mission Supply Co., which was the buying entity for Gov-Mart. Mission Supply was a nonprofit holding company with half of its membership income going to a charity fund administered by a police chief, a judge, and other notables from the community.

Seeing a need for continued expansion of the operation, Joe and his partner constructed a Gov-Mart gas station with sixteen pumps across the street from the Trianon Ballroom store. Something over 600,000 gallons of gasoline, an unheard-of amount for that time, was dispensed at discount prices to members every month. Gov-Mart also began an attempt to rent cars belonging to Budget Rent A Car from its Tacoma outlet at the insistence of Joe Diamond and over the objections of his rent-a-car partner, Johnny Cain. That venture proved fruitless. Nobody is right 100 percent of the time. To this day, Joe believes that if the availability of rental cars had been marketed more enthusiastically, the venture would have reaped great rewards in that area.

Competition was getting nasty. Spies were stationed near the loading platform of Gov-Mart's shipping and receiving department. They were busily, though furtively, writing down the numbers that appeared on the boxes being delivered there. The competitive companies who hired the spies would then contact the suppliers of the numbered merchandise and, using whatever pressure they could exert, try to get deliveries stopped.

Having been made aware of this despicable and unfair practice, Joe simply instructed that the merchandise be repackaged in unmarked cardboard cartons. Case closed.

Despite Gov-Mart's many successes, Joe's partner wanted to sell out and move on to other businesses. Joe didn't have the time to operate this thriving business by himself, being fully involved in a burgeoning law practice, so reluctantly he and his partner both sold out.

Eventually, Gov-Mart's subsequent owner allowed anyone to buy from the store without having to become a member. The membership concept was gone. Gov-Mart exists only in the memories of some of the loyal, old-timer customers as it ultimately succumbed to much larger chains with name recognition everywhere.

Today, Costco is the king of the membership discount department stores, having updated many of the concepts originating with Gov-Mart. Costco's very first outlet anywhere was on 4th Avenue South in Seattle and was undoubtedly patterned somewhat after Gov-Mart and similar operations. With Jerry Alhadeff being one of the original investors in Jeff Brotman's Costco, what could be more natural?

MEMORIES

"During the summer of 1959, one Sunday afternoon, Joe asked me if I would like to go to work for him and my future father-in-law as a floorwalker (trainee) at the Gov-Mart store which they were in the process of building in South Tacoma. He explained I would be trained as the assistant manager for a new store near McCord Air Force Base.

"He offered me a starting salary of $750 per month. I was currently working for my family in the seafood business, making $450 a month. I had recently requested a raise and was promptly informed I was not worth the present salary.

"I asked Joe's permission to discuss the offer with my father. My dad said Joe was crazy, and I should take the offer. I reported for work on September 1, 1959, and because of a bizarre series of events, shortly

thereafter became the manager of the new Tacoma store. Diamond and Shulman enjoyed a tremendous success with their acquisition—sold the stores to Bill Triplett (Big "C" of Portland, Oregon). I stayed on— became general manager of the two stores, and built three additional new stores in Seattle, Renton, and Burien. In 1965 I gave notice and returned to the fish business.

"And that reminds me of my favorite story about Josef that I was a part of: In the fall of 1960 I received a call from Joe. He indicated he was about to take a business trip to San Francisco with his wife, Violett. The purpose was to become involved in NACO (National Association of Consumer Organizations), a group of discount department store owners from throughout the United States. Joe indicated that his wife was ill and he was leaving the next morning, and would I accompany him in her place.

"I gathered—literally—a file drawer of documents to prepare myself and met Joe at the plane. Upon arrival at the Fairmont Hotel in San Francisco in front of the lobby registration desk (you can picture me— a young executive, arms loaded, anxious to get to my first meeting), Joe said, 'Relax—have a good time—I will see you in a couple of days!' I attended a couple of sessions, found them a complete waste of time, and spent the remaining hours with Joe, discussing parking lots, parking lot equipment, and real estate in general.

"Joe was a mentor, unbelievable motivator, and most importantly, a close friend. Many years and many deals after Gov-Mart we became partners in small ventures, and on one very special day, Joe telephoned me. He had heard I was going to Chicago on business. He asked if I would like *to take a pretty lady to dinner—the pretty lady picked me up. We had a delightful evening, and she is now Mrs. Josef (Muriel) Diamond."*

– Jerry Alhadeff

"In Singapore, Joe, with his love for wanderlust, would not stick to the beaten path when we went looking for a restaurant and insisted on getting a cab and finding 'some restaurant where they serve what the real people eat.' We found this place by a combination of pig latin, English and waving our hands and were deposited in front of this neighborhood restaurant as I saw it.

"We entered the place and lo and behold—nobody spoke English. However, we were finally seated and by some method we ordered—all family style. It all looked good and I, being very hungry, pitched in. One dish was especially attractive to me, which later I found to be pressed duck. It was the one dish that I was concentrating on as it was delicious. The food had been deep-fried in a coating. I had one large morsel that I was about ready to pop into my mouth when I looked across the table at Joe and Vi and noticed, to my consternation, that their faces seemed to be turning green. Joe reached across the table and pushed my hand away from my mouth. I looked down at the morsel and my hand and discovered that I was looking at the duck's head. Bill, eyes and all. I had nearly eaten it!

"For the balance of the trip, we all insisted that we stick to restaurants where people at least spoke English and we knew what were ordering and eating. This was just one of the truly memorable occasions involving the single most important friend of my life."

– Donald Macri, Sr.

CHAPTER FIFTEEN
HIS THIRD LOVE

Budget Rent A Car began to grow at a rapid pace. Not only was the company growing in Seattle, but around the country competitors were taking notice. Joe began to cast his eye in the direction of Tacoma as our first natural expansion. For a very short time, we tried to operate that lucrative city as a satellite office with our own employees but quickly realized that we weren't attacking the market as aggressively as it deserved, so the thought of creating a sub-franchise there as a necessary next step came into being.

Among Joe's many parking association friends was Bob Medved, a highly successful and well-respected parking lot operator in Tacoma. Bob was aggressive and, like Joe, always looking for new opportunities. After all, Medved, a good Catholic, needed to provide for his wife, Shirley, and their twelve children. The offspring count might have stopped at eleven, but with her last pregnancy, Shirley managed to produce twins.

Bob had become aware of the tiny Budget operation in Tacoma, and he showed some interest. Without a doubt, he must have been able to see that he could do a far better job of promotion than our employees were doing, as he was well known in the business community there. In one of the meetings of the parking association, Medved and Joe got together, and a deal was made with very little difficulty. Our franchise at the time, for which we paid fairly handsomely, was for the entire State of Washington. Knowing that company growth was more important than money in hand, Joe *gave* the Tacoma area to Bob—free of charge! No up-front payment and no franchise fees over and above what we, as the prime licensee were obligated to pay Budget Rent A Car Corporation.

That arrangement proved to be one of the most important steps we took in our early Budget days. With Seattle-Tacoma International Airport located almost exactly halfway between the cities, the two operations fed off each other. Our Seattle customers were Bob Medved's Tacoma customers and vice versa. Medved caused rapid growth in the Tacoma area as Joe intuitively knew he would. Budget was off and running there as it was in Seattle. Our growth had just begun.

Later in 1963, we became aware that the Budget operators in Portland weren't jumping up and down with joy over their Oregon Budget franchise. The solution to their problem was simple—we bought 'em. Now we became Budget Rent A Car of Washington-Oregon, Inc., and things began popping with Joe's interest being piqued and with Johnny Cain's natural sparkplug attitude. Spokane was added, as was Eugene in Oregon along with various satellite stations in select areas (our small army of dedicated employees capable of properly running these satellites had been growing too), as well as throughout Seattle.

Did we do everything right in Portland, Spokane, and Eugene? Decidedly not. We installed management teams who were supervised almost entirely by phone. John Cain saw supervisory travel to these out-of-town facilities as a waste of money and a boondoggle day off for the traveling supervisor. As general manager of the two-state operation, at one point I had a hopeless drunk operating our Spokane facility and a capable but womanizing man in charge of our Portland operation, and in both cases I was instructed to leave them alone while being required to answer for their profit-and-loss statements. Talk about a recipe for failure! As time went along, however, we corrected those problems with more astute managers, better and frequent supervisory visits, and, of no small consequence, finally the good judgment to subfranchise both Eugene and Spokane. There is no better formula for success than having the owner, whose money is at stake, running an operation.

In order to service arriving airline passengers at Seattle-Tacoma airport, we had made an arrangement with a service station operator whose business was in the middle of the only ingress/egress airport road at the time. We had agreed with him to pay a fee for each car rented and returned to his facility plus another fee for each car washed, serviced, and made ready for the next customer. A reserved customer, who had been "qualified" over the phone by us, would arrive and, as instructed, would call the phone number of the service station. A car would be dispatched to pick him or her up in front of the baggage claim area. The customer and driver would return to the station, where the customer would then sign the rental document and be on their way. The attendants at the service station were not required to qualify the customer or, for that matter, even smell their breath. All but the breath smelling was up to us to do by telephone conversation, which in most cases was as close as our Budget personnel came in contact with the customer. Hazardous? Yes, but we got pretty good at it. It's always amazing what people can do when they have to.

There came a time, however, when Seattle-Tacoma airport thought we should have to pay them some kind of a fee since the service station was on their property and a transaction was being completed there when the customer signed the rental agreement. Once Joe had them committed to the position that the "transaction" revolved around customer's signing a document on airport property, we simply quit having them sign there. We did everything over the phone with the single exception of physically delivering the car and accepting its return. Hard to believe now that we delivered a rental car to a customer whom we'd never met, had only had a telephone conversation with, and without a signature. We even made out the rental document at our downtown Seattle office and asked the customer to come by at his convenience to sign it. Did we have problems with it, you ask? Yes, a few, but for the most part, it worked.

Not to be outmaneuvered, Port of Seattle (airport) officials then began to apply pressure to the service station operator, making his life difficult. Then came the call on a Sunday morning. It was our friend with the service station. He informed us that the airport management had given him 24 hours to get our cars out of there or his lease agreement with them would be in jeopardy. We got the job done in time.

Every car that exited the airport had to travel due east on "airport drive," past the service station from which we had previously, precariously run our insignificant amount of business, to intersect with Highway 99 (previously known as Pacific Highway South and now named International Boulevard) and then north toward Seattle or south toward Tacoma.

Directly across Highway 99 was a swampy area known as Bow Lake, which was owned by the Boysen family. They made a fine living dredging humus soil from that "lake" and selling it to gardeners and landscapers. Bow Lake humus was known far and wide, and it was rare indeed not to see a lineup of pickups and cars with trailers getting loaded with this rich, black soil. The family also owned much of the property across from present-day Seattle-Tacoma International Airport that is now home to several high-rise office buildings, hotels, and parking lots. The upper level of the property directly across Highway 99 from the airport exit extended back about 200 feet and then dropped off sharply to the swampy Bow Lake.

Joe wanted that property for our car rental operation. The Boysen brothers were getting a little tired of slogging around in the swamp all day long anyway, so he arranged a long-term lease with them for the entire property—upper and lower levels. We built our airport office there and erected a massive billboard that could be seen from aircraft holding at 3,000 feet. The sign was BIG! It was so big that a local adversarial columnist for the *Seattle Times* called it a "green monstrosity." It appeared green at certain times of the day because the lettering was made up of those little glittering, shimmering ovals (about double the size of silver dollar) so popular at the time. And, as you might have guessed, it featured "$5 a day and 5 cents a mile" in shimmering letters 10 feet high, along with the orange and black Budget Rent A Car logo and, something very new at the time, AIRPORT PARKING.

We couldn't park many customers cars on the upper level with much of the space during weekends being taken up with our rental cars, so we filled in Bow Lake. A few hundred truckloads of fill dirt did the trick—the south end of Bow Lake became a thriving parking lot.

Our airport business began to flourish as the customers of $10 a day and 10 cents a mile, budget-conscious Hertz, Avis, and National (whom I had dubbed Ol' Yeller, Big Red, and the Green Wienie) were forced to aim their vehicles toward our "green monstrosity" sign and find out that they were paying a premium for service within the airport as opposed to making a phone call and having a car delivered (and their luggage handled) within three to five minutes of their phone call, depending upon traffic.

Something else happened to our tremendous advantage that we couldn't have anticipated. We found that the off-airport parking business dovetailed beautifully with our rental car business. At peak times during the week, when most of our rental fleet was out, parking customers traveling to other destinations filled our lot well. On weekends, our rental fleet was largely idle, but the parking customers had picked up their cars to spend the weekend with their family. We couldn't have asked for a better fit.

I wouldn't presume to say that nobody else had given much thought to the airport parking/car rental combination business, but it is notable that many very similar operations began to crop up around the country.

In the meantime, Budget Rent A Car Corporation had grown exponentially. Many of the early franchisees were becoming quite wealthy, and Budget had become a force to be reckoned with around the world.

Joe Diamond's advice and counsel were not only being sought after by the home corporation, but he and some other highly respected franchise operators were instrumental in creating a Licensee Advisory Board for the purpose of conferring with corporate officers over advertising and operational matters. The best of the best of Budget operators participated as advisory board members. There were, as memory serves, no more than a dozen members of the board, and their thoughts and assistance in approving and endorsing new programs and advertising efforts was of critical importance to other licensees around the country and had much to do with the exciting growth of the Budget system.

One of the advertisements prior to the Licensee Advisory Board coming into being that particularly annoyed Joe was one with the slogan "Prudent People Save a Buck With Budget." Joe objected loud and long, "What is this Prudence Penny nonsense?"

Not long after the Licensee Advisory Board was established, Joe was elected to chair that group and remained in that position for a number of years. Many awards were presented to our Washington/Oregon operations and to Joe Diamond and Johnny Cain individually. I don't think it is too boastful to say that we in Washington and Oregon were looked upon as one of the crown jewels of the Budget Rent A Car System.

I would be remiss not to mention that during this time, Budget Rent A Car in Canada became and remains to this day number one over Hertz and all the others in the industry in that country. Budget in Hawaii and Australia also remain on top of the industry, as is the case with Budget in other parts of the world, including some offices in South Africa, Europe, England, Asia, and the list goes on.

In the meantime, we in Washington and Oregon had added a few sublicensees and offices being run by our own employees. Some of these offices were being run quite successfully and others with not such glowing results. Then came Jerry Costacos. Joe and Johnny Cain decided to take on a 20 percent partner, and Costacos was brought in.

Jerry was with a highly competitive, local in nature, car rental company and had close friends operating franchises for that same company in cities pretty much all over Eastern Washington. When he joined our corporation, his friends and compadres brought their own operations under the Budget flag as well. With the addition of his group of sublicensees, Budget became the best-represented rental car company in Washington State. At peak, we either owned or were advisors to 33 car and truck rental facilities in the states of Washington and Oregon. We had Costacos (who still operates a satellite station at 4th and Columbia in Seattle) to thank for that somewhat overnight growth.

The name Joe Diamond is well-known around the globe but particularly in the United States, where he has had such a great influence over the success of the system.

After a few years of operating our ever more successful car rental service across the highway from Seattle and Tacoma's rapidly growing airport, over the intense objections of Budget Rent A Car Corporation, our home office in Chicago, and somewhat following the lead of Morris Mirkin in Los Angeles (who, by the way, was the founder of Budget Rent A Car) we began to move toward becoming an in-airport operator. That simply meant that we would have a Budget counter in the airport so we could be seen by arriving passengers as they waited to hear that their luggage had been lost … only kidding.

We were fought every step of the way by the "Big Three" (Hertz, Avis, and National) and, it appeared, by the Port of Seattle itself. They cited "not enough room" for an additional operation and other similar excuses for not allowing us to be present within the airport. During that time Dollar Car Rental was also pursuing an in-airport position.

The end result was a combined effort by Dollar and Budget in a lawsuit to force the issue. In a long-fought battle, we came out on top and opened the door not only to ourselves but, as any present-day traveler knows, to many other car rental operations. Arriving customers in the early days had only three choices of car rental companies. These days the choices are almost unlimited.

While Joe always considers himself first and foremost a lawyer, the family business, Diamond Parking, is close to his heart. Budget Rent A Car became, over time, his third love and occupied much of his time and benefited from his closeness to the operation.

MEMORIES

Dorothy Boysen [Fred Boysen's wife—he died in 1988], Ted Boysen, and Rose Boysen wrote: "We first met Joe in 1963 when negotiating the lease for the Budget parking lot across from Sea-Tac Airport at the Bow Lake Humus Co. property, which we own. We worked the lease through our family lawyer, Hans Otto Giese. Joe and he were great contemporaries, having attended the U. of W. law school and shared rides and studies together.

"They were great pals and enjoyed their often heated discussions as well as respect for each other's keen minds. There was much camaraderie and one-upmanship. Neither would permit the other to keep him waiting. They were men of honor and integrity. Many of our agreements were settled with a handshake—their word was their bond.

"Otto owned and sailed the king of Norway's six-meter sailing boat, and I'm sure Joe went sailing on it many times with him. We are proud to have known them and enjoyed their keen minds and friendship."

"Joe was chairman, and I was one of the original members of the [Budget] Licensee Advisory Board. Many times I remember Joe saying to Belzberg [president of Budget Rent A Car Corporation], "Now,

Morris," etc. etc. This had a soothing effect on the entire group, and Belzberg recognized that the entire group was likely to agree with Joe's thinking. This was one of the ways that Joe helped increase my company's profits and, in the long run, its total value, from which I enjoy a pretty good lifestyle today."

– Jim Brooksbank
A highly successful Budget Rent A Car licensee

Another highly successful Budget licensee, Aaron Ferer, wrote: "I first met Joe in San Francisco at the Budget convention when I was put on the advisory board.

"What I think I remember most about Joe was that first meeting where Lenny Solomon [another Budget licensee] was coming off the wall. We actually had a private meeting. Lenny, Joe, me, and Morris Belzberg were in a suite, having breakfast. Lenny, as he was known to do, was in the process of having a major fit. I had never seen anything like this before in my life. Here's Morris Belzberg, the president of Budget, and Lenny is talking to him like he's some kind of mobster. I thought there was going to be blood on the floor or someone thrown out a window. I was not yet 30 years old, this was my first Budget convention, and I was scared. Then I noticed Joe sitting there calmly taking all this in— as if it was routine. I was worried—looking to Joe for some guidance. Joe said a few words and the situation started to calm down.

"That was the first time I saw the 'Great Negotiator' in action. I was so impressed. Then I found that Morris and Lenny did this all the time. Being a young man, I certainly was impressionable. These three men were bigger than life.

"Josef is now one of my dearest friends and I cherish that friendship."

"It was Sunday, May 1, 1977, and it was my first day on the job at Budget. The setting was the Budget International Convention at the Continental Plaza in Chicago. Morris Belzberg, the president of Budget, introduced me to Joe and made some comment about how we had been trying (unsuccessfully) to buy Joe's Budget operations for Washington and Oregon. But we couldn't agree on the price, which was $2–3 million.

"Joe simply smiled and said, 'I'm not interested in selling.' Belzberg and Harvey [Jim Harvey was president of Transamerica] later told me that buying Diamond's Budget franchise was now my challenge. They had both struck out on several occasions. I could hardly wait to get at Diamond. I had negotiated over 100 business deals at Ford Motor Co., and as a lawyer, I felt I had an edge because Joe and I 'talked the same language.' Boy, was I in for a jolt. Joe had negotiated thousands of deals and left behind so many bloody, bent, or broken negotiators and lawyers that he was already a legend. So, shortly after my arrival at Budget, I made what would be the first of many attempts to buy Budget Washington/Oregon.

"Each time the price went up, and although each time seemed like this time we'd do it, Joe would always find some reason to say no. I began to look on Diamond and buying Budget Washington/Oregon as job insurance. I'd try every year or two. Joe would say no, and soon it would be time for me to retire. But then a strange thing happened: Joe turned 80 and concluded he had only about 40 or 50 more years to live and decided he wanted to spend more time with his new bride, Muriel.

He called and said, 'Here's my price—take it or leave it.' I said, 'Joe, what about my job insurance?' Joe agreed to talk to Belzberg about my career, and I agreed to Joe's price, which was $27 million. See, I told you Diamond is a pushover."

   – Clif Haley, who later became president of Budget Rent A Car

CHAPTER SIXTEEN
REVERSE DISCRIMINATION AND THE UNITED STATES SUPREME COURT

Craig Sternberg, a young lawyer in Joe's law offices, asked Joe if he had any objection to suing his alma mater, the University of Washington. Taken aback, Joe hesitated. "I certainly wouldn't be delighted with the prospect of suing them, but if they've wronged someone, I would be willing to take them on."

Sternberg explained that a young friend of his, Marco DeFunis, had been twice denied admission into the University of Washington law school because the class was full. The wrong being perpetrated by the U of W law school was that less qualified minority students were being admitted, while DeFunis, with nearly a 4.0 average, was being told to apply again next year.

Sensitive to and vehemently against discrimination of any kind, Joe agreed to interview Sternberg's young friend.

Sitting across from Joe's large desk in a beautifully furnished office with a sweeping view of Seattle and Elliott Bay, DeFunis began. "I just don't understand it, Mr. Diamond. I graduated from the University of Washington Phi Beta Kappa with almost a four-point average. The law school turned me down and told me to apply next year." He continued, "I waited another year and I applied again. They told me the same thing. How can that be? I had the qualifications and the grades."

Joe listened intently as DeFunis went on with his story. "So, I applied at the University of Oregon. They were willing to accept me right away, but my wife is working as a dental assistant in Seattle, and having been a student for several years, and with little money, I felt I couldn't afford to pick up and move to Oregon to go to law school there.

"There came a point," DeFunis went on, "when I began to realize that something was amiss. How could it be that one school would readily accept my application while the other continued to put me off to next year."

"Did you take just four years at the University of Washington?" Joe asked. "No, after I was turned down the first time at the law school, I signed up for a graduate course, where I received almost a four-point average again," Marco answered.

Joe was convinced, at that point, that Marco DeFunis had a better record than many, if not most, of the students admitted to the University of Washington's law school, in addition to which he was born and raised in Washington State.

"I'll be happy to look into the matter, Marco," Joe said, much to the relief of DeFunis. Nothing was said at that point about a fee, and it was not until now known by very many that Joe Diamond handled the entire lawsuit pro bono.

That same day, Joe phoned Harold Sheffelman, chairman of the Board of Regents at the University of Washington and told him that he would like to talk about young Marco DeFunis. Sheffelman was not only a fellow lawyer but also one of Joe's many friends. After hearing a bare outline of the problem DeFunis was having with the university, Sheffelman advised Joe to discuss the matter with the dean of the University of Washington law school first.

In the dean's office by appointment a few days later, Joe heard, "We're not going to do anything, Mr. Diamond." Incredulous, Joe asked, "Why not?" "Because not only was the class full when Marco applied," responded the dean, "but we had selected the candidates whom we thought were the best. We even included 17 minority students."

A little light blinked on in Joe's mind. "Is it possible that I could see the qualifications of the students who were admitted that year?" Joe asked. "Why on earth would you want to see them?" the stately dean inquired. "Because I want to know if their grades were as good as DeFunis's grades were," Joe replied.

The dean's frame noticeably stiffened as his assistants silently shook their heads no. "Absolutely not!" the dean announced after a moment or two of a pregnant silence. After thanking the dean for his time, Joe departed, concluding that his next move would be to once again discuss the matter with Sheffelman and the regents.

A day or two later he was in the board room of the regents who listened to Joe's comments while seated at a very large oval table. The message that he got from the regents was, "We can't do anything for you about DeFunis." "Well, you leave me with no choice but to sue the University of Washington," Joe informed them matter-of-factly. "Marco is entitled because of his almost perfect grade point average to be admitted to the law school, and I'm going to do my best to see that he is."

As Joe began the lawsuit against the University of Washington during the summer of 1971, the deadline for closing acceptance to the next class was rapidly approaching. Time was of the essence. Appearing in the courtroom, Joe was successful in having Judge Thompson issue a restraining order to stop the university from mailing out acceptance notices to any of the applying students. He knew that the restraining order would buy his client the necessary time to continue the case.

Jim Wilson, the attorney for the University of Washington, cajoled, "Let's not stop the class, Joe. Your injunction will have the effect of holding up the whole class." "That's easy to fix" was Joe's response, "All you have to do is to save a place in the class for my client and then go ahead with your preparations for the class."

After a brief consultation with some of the university hierarchy, Wilson finally agreed: "Okay. We'll commence with our preparations for the class and send out the acceptance letters while holding one space open for a student." The result was that the university allowed Marco DeFunis to attend the law school while the litigation was pending without officially admitting him into the class. After applying for an early court date, Joe and his client were finally in court a week after classes had begun.

Prior to the trial, Joe had requested records of the 149 other students who had been admitted to the class DeFunis was attending. The University of Washington refused to release those records. Joe subpoenaed the records through Judge Shorett's court, and they were delivered to the courthouse and sent to an adjacent room. By this time, the trial was well under way, and the only time that Joe had to review those records was during recess.

During one of these recesses, Joe found ample evidence to present before the court. The files were marked "Admitted" or "Denied." Within the folders, he found handwritten notes on the applications. An example of several that he reviewed was a note such as, "Don't believe she can make it, but let's give her a chance anyway." That file had to do with a female applicant with a 2.5 grade point average, three kids, no income, no husband, and no law background. It was painfully obvious that the school was admitting academically challenged students while holding back one with a 3.9 grade point average and a Phi Beta Kappa to his credit. And this was only one example of at least 15 poorly qualified student applicants that the law school was accepting over Marco DeFunis.

As the evidence was presented before Judge Shorett, he ruled in favor of Joe's client and ordered that he be formally admitted to the class. He was.

One would think that Judge Shorett's ruling would have concluded the matter, but the University of Washington appealed the ruling and it was then sent to the State of Washington Supreme Court in Olympia, the capital. It took nearly a year for the Supreme Court's decision, but the majority of the justices, in a divided opinion, reversed Judge Shorett's decision. It held that the university had the right to make their own rules as to who should be admitted and that they could deny admission to Marco DeFunis.

By the time of the Supreme Court ruling, DeFunis had completed his first year in law school, but Joe was concerned that the University of Washington would kick him out of the second year. To keep him in school, Joe sought a restraining order from the United States Supreme Court. Appearing before Justice William O. Douglas to request the restraining order, Joe was successful. The restraining order was issued.

Having been granted the injunction, DeFunis was allowed to continue in the class while Joe waited for a court date. In order to be heard before the United States Supreme Court, he had to request a writ of certiorari, but before a response to that request was provided, he received a letter from the U.S. Supreme Court inquiring as to whether the case was moot. The year was 1973, and DeFunis had by that time completed two years of the course. However, the course was three years long, and Joe so informed the United States Supreme Court. He advised that the case was not moot and that without the reversal of the State Supreme Court's ruling, the university might opt to kick DeFunis out of the class before he had completed it. The U.S. Supreme Court advised all of the parties that the case would be set for trial. The *Washington Post* would describe it as "the year's most explosive civil rights case."

Eight more months would go by before Josef appeared before the justices in Washington, D.C. By this time, DeFunis had only three weeks before he would graduate with his class. Since there was so little time left, the justices, once again, asked Joe if the case was not, now, moot. Once again, Joe answered no.

Even though DeFunis had only three weeks remaining before graduation, Joe asserted that DeFunis could still be legally kicked out of the class before graduation if the Washington State Supreme Court's ruling was not overturned. So, the case continued. Slade Gorton, the attorney general for the state of Washington had taken over the task of representing the state in place of Jim Wilson, the assistant attorney general. The U.S. Supreme Court granted extra time to Gorton and Joe to prepare to have the matter heard.

Thirty-one amicus briefs were filed—mostly on behalf of the various law schools around the country—which took the position that law schools should have the right to determine who will be admitted to their schools on whatever basis the individual law school deemed right.

Arguing the case, Attorney General Gorton told the Supreme Court of the United States that no matter what they decided, the University of Washington would not kick DeFunis out of the class. Joe's primary goal of getting DeFunis through the law school had been realized regardless of the justices' decision. A victory!

Justice Thurgood Marshall began to question Joe, "Weren't the minorities who were being admitted just as capable as DeFunis?" He continued, "Didn't they all have just as good qualifications?" "No they were not, Your Honor," responded Joe. "Yet they were qualified to law school, were they not?" the justice prodded. "They may have been qualified," Joe answered, "but they weren't the *best* qualified."

The justice's questions came in an almost rapid-fire order, not allowing Joe to present his case in the way he wished to present it. He offered, "Since we are short of time, I would like to finish my argument in an orderly manner, and then I would be pleased to answer any and all questions." He presented his case for DeFunis and then respectfully said, "Now, if you will ask your question again, Justice Marshall, I will be glad to answer."

"I don't need to have any more questions answered from you." was the testy comment from Justice Marshall. End of session.

The decision of the high court came down long after Marco DeFunis had graduated. Their ruling was that a ruling was no longer necessary as the student was no longer in school. They threw it back in the lap of the State Supreme Court. Sound a little like they were trying to avoid taking on the sensitive subject? Could be you're right.

The matter was set for a rehearing in the Washington State Supreme Court. Joe was somewhat perplexed. He was supposed to go back to reargue his case but reargue for what? DeFunis had his diploma. Then, because of his abhorrence of discrimination of any kind, a plan of action came to him. He petitioned the State Supreme Court to make the rehearing a class action suit. That would make the case one to decide the issue for all people in the same or similar situation.

Before the court, Joe pled, "I want to make this a class action suit and have you decide it. If you decide against me again, it will simply confirm that you are consistently wrong. It doesn't really make much difference how you rule," he continued, "because whichever way you decide, if you make it a class action lawsuit as I've requested, it will go right back before the United States Supreme Court, and they will have to make a final decision."

Presiding Judge Finley asked, "What authority is there for this court to make this a class action this late in the proceedings?" "I have been unable to find any authority to make this a class action," Joe answered, "but I can't find anything that says it can't either. This court can do anything it wants to in this matter if there isn't any authority to the contrary." Joe went on, "There's nothing to prevent you from making this a class action."

Interrupting, Assistant Attorney General Jim Wilson, representing the university for this proceeding, asked the court to reinstate its previous decision. "You want us to us to reaffirm our previous decision, which the Supreme Court of the United States reversed and said we were wrong?" Judge Finley asked incredulously, "How can we do that?"

The Washington State Supreme Court decided nothing. It was over. Marco DeFunis had his doctorate of law degree and passed the bar exam. He became a highly successful personal injury lawyer in Seattle. In January 2002, at the age of 52, Marco DeFunis died.

Four years after the success of the Marco DeFunis case, Joe responded to an inquiry from a lawyer in California. A case very similar to the DeFunis case had come up there. A white Vietnam veteran, Allen Bakke, was being denied enrollment in the University of California Medical School. The California lawyer requested copies of Joe's briefs on the DeFunis case and, along with others, used those briefs as the basis for another Supreme Court challenge of the same issue. The Supreme Court of the United States ruled in favor of Bakke.

The DeFunis and Bakke cases are now being used in law schools across the country.

MEMORIES

From Marco DeFunis, this writing, "Craig Sternberg was a young associate in the firm of Lycette, Diamond and Sylvester and agreed to suggest to Joe that he help me with my admission to law school at the University of Washington. I, frankly, was extremely intimidated to meet this man who was represented to me as one of the most powerful attorneys in the city of Seattle. I was very pleased to note that he had a wonderful smile, a great handshake and a twinkle in his eye that was willing to take on the establishment.

"And that reminds me of my favorite story about Josef that I was part of: As the DeFunis trial against the University of Washington was coming to a close, it just so happened that the Jewish holiday of Rosh Hashana was occurring. Being orthodox, I was required to celebrate two days of the holiday. It also happened that, through Joe's legal tactics, a seat was reserved for me alone at the law school and could not be filled until the trial was concluded.

"Joe had an afternoon conference with the attorney for the University of Washington and the judge and discovered in that conference that the

law school's orientation was going on. The judge, Lloyd Shorett, was a very tall, silvery-haired individual who had apparently told Joe that he recommended that I attend one of the days of orientation that the trial would be recessed for.

"Joe came to me with a smile on his face like the cat that ate the canary, and said, 'I think it might be a good idea if you went to to orientation on the second day of Rosh Hashana. I am not saying that the judge is going to rule in your favor, but I do feel it would be a good idea if you went.' Well, so much for praying. I did as I was instructed. After all, when Joe told you something, you simply did it.

"As the trial came to a conclusion and before the judge rendered his opinion, I had feared that additional adverse testimony might come in that would make it difficult if not impossible for the trial to be won. Fearing the worst, I drove to Eugene, Oregon, where I had been accepted in the University of Oregon law school, reserved an apartment, reserved a rental truck for the move down, and was ready to pay my tuition. Joe, in his most conservative manner, offered no consolation. In fact, he had also had some concerns about the outcome. The day the decision was rendered, we all met outside the courtroom; my mother, father, mother-in-law, father-in-law, sister, brother-in-law occupied the first couple of rows in the courtroom.

"The judge made his ruling, and the course of legal history in Washington was changed. Several years later, and many pages of briefing, legal research, and documentation having been performed, the Supreme Court decided to declare the case moot. But despite all of that, I shall never forget that sly grin."

CHAPTER SEVENTEEN
NORTHWEST BANK

It was an ad in the *Wall Street Journal* that started it. Living in Phoenix, Somers White's friend told him that he saw an ad for an executive for a bank that was being started in Seattle.

Somers was a young man who had graduated from Amherst College, had enrolled in Chase Manhattan Bank's Executive Training Program for nearly a year, left that program to continue his education at Harvard Business School, and had gone on to work in the banking industry in Phoenix. Reasonably successful at his young age, he was still looking for a larger responsibility. Then came his friend's comment about the ad.

A new bank was in the works in Seattle, the dream child of Jim Harms of Harms Transport fame. The newly seated board of directors, including one Joe Diamond, had placed an ad in the *Journal,* looking for bank executives. Joe's position on the board was secretary, director, and general counsel. Somers responded to the ad by mail and provided his résumé. Soon he was called and asked to come to Seattle for an employment interview. The caller asked what position he was applying for and he responded, "president." An appointment was set up. The year was 1961.

There were 487 applicants, some with well-known names in the banking industry and with titles such as vice president and senior vice president of various banks around the country. Our man, Somers, showed up, gave a flip-chart presentation, and was hired. He tells us that, to this day, he doesn't know how many, if any, of the other applicants were interviewed. He had become the youngest president of a bank in a large, metropolitan area in the country.

So, the new president of the not-yet-opened Northwest Bank was in place, and it fell to him to work through the process of staffing the new operation and putting together the charter. Early on he was warned by Harms that one of the directors, Joe Diamond, was tough and hard to deal with. He soon found that entirely the opposite was the case. He found Diamond to be easy to deal with and very persuasive. Somers reminded himself of the comment Mikhail Gorbachev had made about Ronald Reagan, "The most persuasive individual I have ever been with." He thought that comment could easily have been made about Joe Diamond.

No new bank charters had been issued in Seattle since the one to Bill Boeing in 1934. One person commented that Seattle was underbanked and overbranched. It seemed that five families controlled all the banking in the Greater Seattle area.

Somers set about putting together the charter, fully aware that it was a daunting task.

Enter one of Joe Diamond's old Garfield High School classmates and good friend, also, as it happens, governor of the state of Washington, Al Rosellini. Governor Rosellini offered to assist in the approval of the charter, and soon it became a reality.

Somers and Joe became close friends almost immediately upon getting to know each other. During his first eight months here (albeit commuting back and forth to Phoenix before he moved his family here), Somers had one meal each day, seven days a week, with his friend Joe Diamond. They talked about everything, not just banking but business philosophies, parking lots, law, loyal employees, and just about everything else was digested along with those enjoyable repasts. Somers says that he learned constantly from Joe during that period. During those months and before a bank office was in place, Joe offered Somers free office space. He accepted gratefully.

A site for the bank was selected. It was in a parking garage owned by Charlie Travers at Third and Pine, across the street from what was then the Bon Marché. Some problem arose having to do with the construction of the garage as it related to the bank occupancy that required some extensive (and expensive) repair before the bank could open.

Joe met with Travers to discuss the matter. "Charlie, if you want the rent to start from the date we signed the lease or a month from now or whatever you decide," Joe offered, "I'll go along." The end result was that the bank had three or four months of free rent after it had officially opened. Joe was indeed the master of persuasion.

One of the first tasks was to sell stock in Northwest Bank. Somers was concerned. He said to Joe, "But I don't know anyone in Seattle." He began, however, to sell stock. His first sale was to a telephone installer. He bought two shares at $50 each. The next day, the IBM salesman agreed to buy 10 shares and the following day brought his father-in-law in to buy $10,000 in stock from Somers. He did fairly well in sales, but by far the biggest seller of shares in the bank was, as you might have guessed, Joe Diamond. He either knew or was in business with almost everyone in town, and because of his reputation for integrity and honesty, he found many willing purchasers. He sold to clients, business associates, rabbis, and friends. His dentist was quick to jump on Joe's bandwagon and purchased stock in the new bank without hesitation.

At the grand opening, in 1963, Somers and Governor Rosellini rode up in an armored car to the festivities including music by a high school band. They were off to a great start except for one small glitch. They had expected to open with $8 million in assets, and it turned out they could only boast $2 million. It was, therefore, pretty hard initially to get depositors.

Somers hired a number of attractive young women as staff and during the grand opening was talking with each of them to make sure that they were offering their assistance to customers wishing to open an account. Joe noticed him scurrying around the room and motioned him over. "You're a bank president now, Somers. You don't have to work so hard."

Northwest Bank, under Somers White's talented leadership, which he was allowed to exercise with a free hand by the directors, started many innovative merchandising programs. One of their depositors was a company that sold pool tables and accessories. A pool table was brought into the bank lobby, and those interested could shoot a game or two in their free time. The Seattle Seafair Committee (Seafair is a weeklong celebration in Seattle, culminating with hydroplane races) put together a promotion where they offered to give away $2,000. Remember, $2,000 was a whole bunch of money in 1963. The promotion was heavily advertised with the information that the money was "hidden" in an obvious place that could be easily seen. Whoever found the $2,000 would be allowed to keep it.

The committee selected Somers's Northwest Bank lobby as their "obvious place." He taped the twenty $100 bills to the windows of the two-story lobby. While the money was readily visible if anyone should direct their eyes upward where it was taped high on the windows, nobody ever saw it. Eventually, it was returned to the Seafair Committee.

Another first ever innovation (at least in the Seattle area) was a Joe Diamond idea. It was night banking. One night a week the bank stayed open until 9:00 p.m. No other bank in Seattle was offering night banking, and the novel offer was quickly and gratefully received by Seattleites not able to get to the bank during regular hours, which in those days were 10:00 a.m. to 3:00 p.m.

Another first: a new approach to banking was the advent of automated data processing. Joe's reasoning for his idea was, "Let's do the accounting for our business customers." The depositors loved it, and not long after, other banks began to adopt the special customer service.

Somers, with some pride in his voice, tells us that every employee of the bank was a stockholder. Many bought in of their own free will, seeing the bank as an investment opportunity, but in addition, at their first Christmas party, each employee was presented with one share of bank stock. Each of the employees looked at Northwest Bank through owner's eyes, and the result was evident in the way customers were handled, and problems that might have otherwise been serious were solved easily and quickly.

An example of that esprit de corps was the time when an elderly gentleman stumbled on the stairs as he entered the bank, fell, and broke his leg. You would think, "Oooops—there's a lawsuit in the making," but it didn't happen. It's hard to know exactly why the customer didn't start a litigation over his injuries, but it might have had something to do with the fact that the attractive young ladies mentioned earlier, without any directive to do so or any encouragement from the bank, visited the old-timer in the hospital every day. At least one of them showed up to see how he was doing each day without fail. Why? Because they liked him.

Northwest Bank exuded excitement and energy. There was always something going on. One promotion Somers came up with was to give away a pony. They kept that pony in a pen in the lobby during the day for two weeks before it was given to a lucky young person. The involved employees took it upon themselves to see to its feeding, watering, and picking up residual deposits.

Somers left to go back to Arizona after a couple of exciting years and was sorely missed by Joe and many others in Seattle. One of Joe's associates in the law office paid Somers a compliment that he remembers vividly to this day. As Somers was getting ready to leave town, Si Wampold shook his hand and said, "I'm so sorry you are going. I cannot begin to tell you what a loss this is to me personally and to the city."

Three years after returning to Arizona, Somers White ran for State Senate and won an election that even his friends said he was bound to lose by a 10-to-1 margin. He won by 2-to-1 over an opponent who headed the largest single political organization in Phoenix. His win was so impressive that Sandra Day O'Connor approached him to run her first political campaign. He did and she won. He developed the motto, "If you believe in Excellence—Vote for it."

Joe and Somers became fast friends, and they keep track of each other on a regular basis even though over 40 years have passed. Once Somers presented Joe with a silver box with the inscription "To Joe Diamond, without whom there would not be a successful Northwest Bank." Joe kept that on his desk over 40 years and recently gave it back to Somers, saying, "I'm not going to be around forever, and I think you should have this to enjoy for the next 40 years."

Why are they such close friends? Somers White's father said it best when he observed, "Joe Diamond is like a second father to you."

In Somers White's very successful book, "Walking with the Wise," he says, "During the director's meeting, I had more and stronger disagreements with Joe Diamond than with any of the other directors, but I never left a meeting without feeling that Joe and I were on the same team and without increased admiration for him.

"I know of numerous instances where Joe Diamond put other people's interests above his own. Joe had a piece of property in downtown Seattle. He leased it to two black men who wanted to start a business at one quarter the price of another offer he had. Joe said, 'I want them to have a chance to succeed.'

"When the bank had a disagreement with the owner of a very small business, Joe Diamond told the bank board of directors, 'I am sorry, but you will have to get another attorney for this case because this woman is my client and her relationship with me goes back further than that of the bank. She needs me more than you do.'"

MEMORIES

Sanford (Sandy) Bernbaum Sr. wrote: "Dear Josef, We were elated to be included in your 'Book of Memories' in honor of your 83rd birthday. We wish you many happy, healthy years with your lovely wife, Muriel, whom we dearly love along with you.

"Our friendship extends over the last 50 years over which time you have been a dear friend. I remember 50 years ago when you bought what was then a very large life insurance policy. You referred me to other clients and were a great center of influence for me.

"I also was pleased to have been nominated by the board, based upon

Senior Director *July 1980*

Attorney Josef Diamond, a Seattle civic and business leader, today was elected a senior director of Old National Bancorp. He has served on the board of the Spokane-based financial services holding corporation since 1970, when it acquired North West Bank, of which Diamond was a director. Old National Bancorp. officials said the vacant position on the board resulting from Diamond's elevation to senior director was filled today by Spokane attorney John Neff. Diamond is board chairman of Washington Mortgage Inc., Eugene Detroit Contractors Inc., Central Wholesale Inc. and Diamond Parking Inc., the latter company the operator of several Diamond Parking lots in Spokane.

your recommendation, of Northwest Bank. The appointment ended up being one of my best investments.

"Carlyn joins me in sending our love and hopes you can live to be 100 so you can eat McDonald's hamburgers, which we know you also love."

"In 1974 when Old National Bank transferred me to Seattle, I met Joe who was then a director for the bank. Joe was very helpful in getting me acquainted in the community, and as my career has changed over the years from ONB to Seattle Trust then Key Bank his support has continued.

– Gordon G. Brandt

"It was about 20 years ago when I first met Joe Diamond, at the time that Northwest Bank merged into the Old National Bank and Joe came on the board of Old National Bank. If first impressions have any bearing on anything, my first impression of Joe Diamond was extremely favorable. He is an utterly charming, warm, and friendly man. His ability to look on the bright side of every situation turned out to be a key element in our ability to recover from a serious financial problem in California.

"With Joe's steadfast support of the ONB management, his timely and thoughtful advice was always welcomed and appreciated. In a lifetime, you are lucky if you meet a handful of people on whom you can really count to come through when the chips are down. Joe Diamond is one of those people, and I consider it a privilege to have known him these past 20 years.

"I wish him many happy returns of the day on the celebration of his 83rd birthday. Although Joe is one who shuns taking credit and is not susceptible to flattery, I think it is time we all insist that he stands up and takes a bow to a standing ovation from his many friends and associates, for whom he has always gone the extra mile."

– David A. Clack

Somers White relates: "I first met Joe Diamond at a meeting of the initial board of directors for the Northwest Bank when they interviewed me for president.

"After I was hired, Joe said, 'You are going to need office space, and we have an extra office in the law offices at the Hoge Building. You can office there at no charge. You will have the advantage that it is next to the men's room, and you will meet just about everybody in the firm.' He was right.

"It was a wonderful experience, as just about every day I had one meal with Joe. Although I graduated from Amherst College and the Harvard Business School, nothing compared to what I learned in those eight months with Joe.

"There are hundreds and hundreds of stories I could tell about Joe Diamond, all of them wonderful. I only wish Joe would write the book about his life which he has talked about, entitled Worry Later.

"My favorite recollection of Joe is his comment, 'I will be glad to do anything, but I just want to be able to tell the world about it.' It is too bad that we can't tell more of the world about the fabulous Joe Diamond and all the wonderful things he has done."

CHAPTER EIGHTEEN
IMPORTING FAD CLOTHES

Norm Ginsberg is 86 years old at this writing and, as Muriel Bach Diamond says, "still refers to Joe as Mr. Diamond." There is a reason for that.

Norm worked with his father for many years in a small but successful business, Electric City, next door to Johnny Cain's Shell station on Olive Street in downtown Seattle. Looking for new opportunities as all true entrepreneurs do, Norm toyed with the idea of importing clothing from the Far East and marketing the goods in and around Seattle. It was 1972.

A problem arose when he found that, while quite successful in his current situation, he simply didn't have enough money to swing the total package that he had in mind. While searching for the necessary funding, he happened on Jim Daly, who was a vice president of what was then the National Bank of Commerce, located in the triangle at the three-way intersection of 7th Avenue, Westlake Avenue, and Olive Street. Daly was not only a friend of Johnny Cain and Josef Diamond, he was also the person who dealt on a day-to-day basis with the Budget Rent A Car account (which later came to be the largest account at that branch) since Budget's downtown office was only half a block away.

Jim Daly suggested that Norm should look to Budget for financing of his operation. He knew Cain and Diamond were always on the lookout for new challenges. A meeting was set, and the result was that a partnership was formed with Norm Ginsberg owning 50 percent of "Budget Importing" while Joe and Johnny each had 25 percent. The partnership agreement was a one-year arrangement just to get things under way. Things indeed got under way. With the signatures of Joe and John on the dotted line with the bank, the importing business was moving, a juggernaut that continued to gain momentum even though the first year showed little, if any, in terms of profit.

Joe had some contacts in the Far East, including his own tailor, Andy Sippy from Hong Kong, who visited Seattle regularly to take orders from Joe and others, most of whom had been referred to Sippy by none other than Joe Diamond. Joe was the kind of man who, if he liked you, would do his best to persuade all of his friends to like you too and to do business with you in whatever your endeavor. One of Joe's favorite little chuckles was to refer to Andy Sippy's wife as Missus Sippy. He got such a kick out of it that one just about had to giggle with him.

As another aside, I was never in any danger of being voted the best dressed man in Seattle, a condition that was likely noticeable to everyone else but not to me. I never had any great interest in clothes. On one of the occasions when Sippy was in town taking orders, Joe suggested that I go to Andy's hotel suite and look at some of his samples. I thought, "Oh well, I'll do it to please Joe," and reluctantly made an appointment. When I arrived, Sippy started taking measurements. I was putting up with the program but had no intention of buying anything—hell, I couldn't afford it. Soon Andy was asking which two suits I would like to order. Two suits? Nonsense! Then he let me know that his friend Joe Diamond wanted to buy two suits for me. I was overwhelmed. I was now the proud possessor of two tailor-made suits.

There was one distressing aspect of the "purchase" of these two suits. Andy Sippy had an ordering form that showed the silhouette of four men. There was the slender one, the barrel-chested one, the one that was kind of round, and the one that was decidedly pear shaped. He circled the latter one on my order. How humiliating!

Back to Budget Importing. So, Joe suggested a trip to the Far East to set up the necessary contacts and suppliers to support the import business. Soon the three novice importers and their wives were on an airplane and across the international dateline with stops scheduled in, among other places, Taiwan and Hong Kong. A supplier was found, and Budget Importing started bringing faux leather jackets

Diamond family home on Lake Washington, circa 1975

and polyester pants and similarly lower-priced items into the Seattle market.

After a year, the fledgling company was showing small promise and Budget's controller, Marilyn Harlan, recommended that the partnership not be continued beyond the original one-year contract. Diamond and Cain didn't disagree, with the result that, after one year, Ginsberg was the sole owner of the importing company along with his wife, Dee. Once again, the problem of undercapitalization reared its ugly head.

Seattle banks, some with quite limited visionary attributes, wouldn't talk with the couple so, undaunted (or at least only slightly daunted), they approached the Hong Kong and Shanghai Bank in Seattle, where they were able to negotiate the necessary business loan.

The couple continued importing quick-sale items and began to do reasonably well. Both of them worked in their somewhat dingy warehouse office, personally unpacking and sorting shipments and arranging for delivery to the retail outlets who were handling their products.

They might have been content to continue with that now profitable venture without change but for the intervention of a Hong Kong businessman, Latchman Narain, who persuaded them to go into the jeans business. The fact that washed denim jeans could become "designer jeans" by simply sewing a logo to

the area that is normally hidden be a seated posterior had been proven by Walter Schoenfeld, chairman of Schoenfeld Industries with its Schoenfeld Neckware, Ltd., subsidiary.

With several pairs of jeans purchased from Nordstrom, in his luggage, Norm settled in once again for the long flight to Hong Kong (a trip that he was to make many times in the coming years). His contact there was able to come up with a manufacturer who would create knockoffs of these very popular items of clothing for export to Ginsberg.

With the borrowed money and the encouragement of their friend Joe Diamond, Norm and Dee began to import the jeans and created a handsome logo of a rose to be embroidered on the hip pocket along with the name Normandee Rose.

Normandee Rose jeans caught on just like the hula hoop and Frisbees. Soon, they were being sold in every upscale shop on the West Coast. They jumped off the racks at Nordstrom, the Bon Marché (now Macy's), the Squire Shop, Jeans Warehouse, and similar retail outlets. Every young person had to have Normandee Rose jeans or they were considered "not cool," a terrible condition for a kid to be in. Being not cool was tantamount to being an outcast. Normandee Rose jeans were the hottest thing on the market in just about every market from Denver west.

With constant input, advice, and encouragement from Joe, Norm and Dee thrived and the revenues continued rolling in.

From gross sales of half a million in 1976, Normandee Rose brought in well over $10 million in 1981 with Dee and Norm and their son, Ron, all fully involved in the business.

Sadly, Norm lost his wife, Dee, a few years ago, and he finally retired a millionaire. Initially he would spend a few of the wetter and colder months of the year in Palm Desert in California but about three years ago made the ultimate move—he lives there year round now in a reasonable degree of luxury within the gates of a country club.

Norm Ginsberg credits Joe Diamond with his success and, as mentioned earlier, continues to call him Mr. Diamond.

MEMORIES

"At his home in Laurelhurst, John Cain, [Joe's] partner in the car rental business arranged a meeting of the three people. We formed Budget Importing Co. and were partners for one year. Mr. Diamond and Mr. Cain, at the urging of their controller, Marilyn Harlan, sold the company to my wife, Dee, and me. We then used the Normandee Rose name and were successful since.

"One year, the three partners along with their wives made a trip to the Far East. A manufacturer problem developed and I was very rude and upset with one of our suppliers. Mr. Diamond observed but made no comment until we arrived in Honolulu on our way back to Seattle. He was staying at the new Halekoa Hotel reserved for retired servicemen and officers. I was in another hotel. He called me and suggested a

breakfast meeting. He has a 'rule' to never argue with a partner. He did not on this occasion, but he did address my shortcomings and temper by explaining to me that the Chinese are very strong people with long memories and explained that I needed to shorten my string and many other of my personalities should be revised to make sure that I understood we, as well as our suppliers, were partners. I have never forgotten this lecture. It helped me from that time forward.

– Norm Ginsberg

In a Seattle Times *local news article from March 17, 2002, staff columnist Nicole Brodeur wrote, in part: "It cost me $7 to meet Seattle parking-lot czar, Joe Diamond: Five dollars for the first hour, and $2 for the five minutes I stayed past that listening to Diamond talk about his good life, made that much better by the money he would get out of me.*

"Still, I had to smile. It's not often you pay someone for the privilege of wishing them a happy birthday.

"Josef Diamond is 95 this month. What that means, he can only describe in physical terms: he can't walk very well and doesn't drive anymore. What that means to his friends: two billboards, erected in his honor, touting his landmark longevity. 'Josef Diamond...95 and going strong!' the billboards applauded from Madison and Broadway and from First and Denny. 'Congratulations, from your friends.'

"The friends, he believes, are people like him: Seattle staples whose family names are engraved into city buildings.

"Diamond has his name on a building—and on the spaces around countless others.

"But even though parking has made him a rich man, he says the lots are 'a sideline' to his vocation as an attorney. Diamond is the oldest practicing lawyer in the state of Washington.

"I wish him well in his corner office on the second floor of the Diamond Building on Elliott Avenue, where he transferred his law office four months ago. On the other side of the door, his son and grandson run the parking business."

CHAPTER NINETEEN
CONSTRUCTION, DEMOLITION, AND DETROIT

One of the more significant happenings in Joe's life was when he met Eugene Detroit. A story of Joe Diamond would not be complete without spending some time talking about his relationship with Gene.

Gene had been and had done just about everything before he met Joe in 1947. Among other things, he had spent time in the merchant marine; had been a miner in the Canadian Yukon territory; had delivered mail by dogsled with his younger brother, Curtis; and had been an amateur hockey player in the Canadian Nationals League, where the best of the best amateurs play in that country.

At the time of his first meeting with Joe in the late 1940s, Gene was working in construction though he had no formal training in that field, being self-taught as he was in his many other endeavors. Joe and Gene, though complete opposites, became as close as brothers and worked together on many projects for the remaining days of Gene's life (Gene died in 2004). He became Joe's confidant and general contractor. They were different in many ways. Joe always took great care to use proper grammar, while Gene abused the English language with impunity. Gene's cavalier approach to the language wasn't a sign of ignorance (as a matter of fact, he had some college in his background). It appeared to be more a case of feeling the need to get a lot said with a very few words. One never had any difficulty knowing where Gene Detroit stood on a given matter. He called 'em the way he saw 'em. Among the other differences, Joe's clothes always gave the impression that they had just been retrieved from the cleaners, while Gene's appearance would lead one to think he had just emerged from a sump or a sawdust pile, which, in fact, many times was the case.

Joe had ultimate trust in Gene Detroit. He was the only person (other than family) who had a key to every property, building, or facility of Diamond Parking, Budget Rent A Car, or any other of Joe's holdings.

It is good to note that Gene watched over Joe's interests zealously. If he knew of a situation or an occurrence that might have an adverse effect on Joe, he reported it immediately. Further, as general contractor, he cut some corners that would have greatly distressed Joe, had he known. I recall one instance where we had acquired an old building (the vacant top floor was known to have been a house of ill repute in the early part of the 20th century) immediately adjacent to the Budget Rent A Car property on the corner of Westlake and Virginia in Seattle. The lower floor was the original home of Underhill's Unfinished Furniture.

Gene Detroit was asked to destroy that old building to enlarge our facility for additional parking and for the construction of a two-story structure that was going to serve as our head-quarters office on the upper floor and small service facility and car wash on the lower floor. Gene and his crew began to demolish the ancient brick structure, and as they began to dismantle the side and back walls (for reasons not clear to me), soon the two-story front wall, facing the street, was left standing precariously. The sidewalk was blocked off, of course, so no pedestrians were endangered, but this tall, brick wall was teetering back and forth in the wind. Located on the sidewalk directly in front of the unstable edifice was a large, gray metal traffic light control box. Gene, seeing my conster-nation over the situation, half-jokingly explained to me the cost we would have to absorb if that wall were to come down and damage the box. As if waiting for its cue, a light gust of wind came along and dropped the several tons of bricks right on top of the box and, as in the old country song about a man with a broken heart, *mashed that sucker flat!*

It was several days later when we learned that particular box was obsolete and had been disconnected long ago in favor of a more modern traffic light control center. We bore no cost, and I'm pretty sure Joe never heard of the near disaster. Gene

Detroit, always aware of the value of plumbing, lighting fixtures, and used brick and copper in buildings being torn down, gathered up all of the unbroken used brick and trucked it out for use in other Diamond construction projects.

Joe relied heavily upon Gene for that and many other reasons. As has been mentioned earlier, Joe's real dream in life was to be an architect, a designer of buildings. He was able to realize that dream vicariously through Gene.

Together, they demolished old, worn-out buildings and built new ones. Many times, the design of the new structure was Josef's. Together, they erected massive billboards throughout the Greater Seattle area (Portland and Spokane were also liberally covered with such advertising media). Though some billboards were leased to other companies, the bulk of them were devoted to Budget Rent A Car.

One of the main themes of this profusion of billboards was to notify car rental customers that with Budget they could avail themselves of FREE parking at ANY Diamond Parking location, and these locations seemed to be only a block or two away from everywhere. The effect was that many people who might otherwise have been renting their car from a well-known competitor were enticed into renting from Budget. Some rental customers actually used Budget's free parking feature to the extent that the free parking more than offset the cost of the rental. Those rental customers were the exception, but the end result was that internal Budget surveys showed that something over 40 percent of their customers were using the service because of the free parking offer. Budget grew at a great rate. The free parking promotion was Joe's brainchild, and it can be said that he didn't receive full cooperation on the idea from some of the local Budget hierarchy but it worked.

Joe Diamond and Gene Detroit made a great team.

Imagine the possibilities in the ...

Symons Building

The Symons Building has been an integral part of Spokane's business community and the home of the *first* local radio station. Located in the heart of downtown and part of the terabyte triangle, with DSL lines and satellite dish networks available.

Imagine what *your* business could achieve.

Imagine the possibilities...

Diamond rules parking empire

By RICHARD RIPLEY

Josef "Joe" Diamond's name probably is displayed more prominently in downtown Spokane than anyone else's. Numerous Diamond Parking Inc. lots dot main arteries in the city's heart, and a sign at each lot bears the Diamond name.

Diamond, 86, is the tenacious chairman of Diamond Parking, a 61-year-old family-owned Seattle company that runs more parking lots here than any other operator.

Diamond Parking owns or manages more than 5,000 parking spaces at its 50-plus locations here, about half of which are in downtown Spokane.

Now the company is angling for more. It's trying to land the concession at the new Spokane Veterans Memorial Arena,

Diamond Parking is seeking growth in Spokane area

Josef "Joe" Diamond, 86, Chairman of Diamond Parking

which is under construction.

So far, however, "that's just a hope," says Joe Diamond. Parking at the old Coliseum, which the arena will replace, is handled now by the city of Spokane.

Joe Diamond still plays an active role in the company's parking empire, even though he's at an age when most people

have long since retired.

During a recent visit here, Diamond inspected some of the company's Spokane lots and met with city officials in Coeur d'Alene, where Diamond Parking runs city-owned lots.

Diamond Parking is the Spokane area's largest operator of scattered parking facilities, although RiverPark Square and the Parkade, which have large garages, probably do more volume, says Dan Geiger, Diamond's Spokane manager.

Some Diamond lots sit squarely in the

See DIAMOND page 22

MEMORIES

"While rejuvenating the Coeur d'Alene Hotel in Spokane, Washington, we were removing an old elevator and planning to install a newer model when we had a bad accident—a fire. The fire broke out in the elevator house, and the shaft was like a chimney. The whole seventh floor, which consisted of a couple of dumpy apartments, a sleeping room, and a large storeroom, was completely gone.

"When the firemen arrived, they extinguished the flames and the fire chief sent half of the crew home when it looked as though they had the fire under control. But shortly after, the flames erupted and finished burning off the seventh floor. We thought the fire was arson for various reasons, but the insurance company's arson investigators stated that the fire was an accident caused by a cutting torch used by an employee.

"Opening day of the Spokane World's Fair, President Nixon opened the show, and we were watching from the rooftop of Joe's famous hotel and

Secret Service people with loaded guns approached us. How they got to the rooftop I do not know. It was exciting for a few minutes. They decided not to chase us off the roof, but they left a couple of servicemen to be with us.

"Memories? There are many more—and if you write a book, I want to be in on it. My life has been a lot of fun and very exciting and interesting. It is now 43 years since I met [Joe]—and when I look back at the years, they were all good.

"Thank you, good Lord, for bringing us together."

— Gene Detroit

[I'm sorry Gene could not have participated in putting together this biography. His input would have been invaluable.]

"My fifteen-year association [with Joe Diamond] produced many wonderful 'stories'—humorously funny, some of them; some of them not so funny. I should have kept a diary.

"Two things that are especially vivid in recall: I remember Joe getting the Harbor Club to "go co-ed" because he liked to lunch there for business meetings, and as he told the club, he had a woman executive in one of his organizations and soon other companies would begin to make the request. I guess I was never properly appreciative, and I still do not have any objection to the boys having their own retreat. It was a milestone, even so.

"What I remember most, though, was Joe's ability to inspire people to perform at their best and to realize their own potential. I learned so much from Joe that I began to refer to him as 'Josef Diamond University,' a title that someone else bestowed but I quickly adopted.

"If anybody is listening, there is much to be learned from our elder statesman—still."

– Marilyn Harlan
Budget Rent A Car controller for many years

CHAPTER TWENTY
THREE BEAUTIFUL WIVES

On the occasion of Joe Diamond's 97th birthday, he and I were in his study, going over several pasteboard boxes of material, most of which was in total disarray, as research for this book.

On a shelf beside his desk were three pictures. The three strikingly handsome women were his three wives. His comment was, "Can you believe that one man can be blessed with three such beautiful women?"

Joe married Violett in 1932. She was the mother of his two children, Joel and Diane. She was the one who made the many moves during Joe's military career to be close to him, along with their children. They were well on their way toward a golden wedding anniversary when Violett (Joe called her Vi) died of cancer on September 4, 1979.

Once, after Joe and Violett had been married for about 25 years, Joe had to go to the island of Truk, in the South Pacific, to settle a legal matter for one of his clients. Though they trav-

Violett Diamond

eled together almost everywhere, on this occasion, for some reason, Joe was unable to take Vi with him.

On his return, Vi proudly announced that while he was gone, she had converted to Judaism. To say he was surprised would be a gross understatement. Joe was dumbfounded. He had no idea that she had aspired to such a thing. She hadn't mentioned it to him. Vi explained that she had asked Rabbi Raphael Levine to convert her, only to hear that he was unable to do so. She then went to Rabbi Singer. "You will have to study up on it," said the rabbi, whereupon he gave her four books on Judaism to read. After having a quick look at the covers, Violett told Rabbi Singer that she had already read three of them. He chuckled when he commented, "You are a better Jew than Joe ever was."

"I could never have found a more wonderful wife than Violett was to me," Joe reminisced later. "We lived together for 47 years without a problem between us. We raised two fine children, each of whom had two fine children of their own. All of them are great. They are college graduates and very successful."

As a loving tribute to Vi's memory, Joe constructed a building on Seattle's "ship canal" near the Seattle Pacific University bearing her name—the Violett Building.

The project architect said, "His objective was that the quality of design and materials be worthy of having his wife's name on it." The architect added, "He also said in his quietly humorous way, 'We do have some ability to help you with the layout of the parking lot.'"

Perhaps this would be an appropriate time to relate a story about just what a classy lady Vi Diamond was. During a certain convention in some exotic location, my wife, Rosie, and I were invited to a very special dinner put on by General Motors. It was one of those banquets where there were four different fine wines at each table—one for each course. We were seated with Vi and Joe Diamond and two other couples. One couple was the GM host and his wife. The other couple I'll call Beulah and Bill. When the entree was served, it was a beautiful filet mignon, perfectly cooked to each diner's specified degree of doneness. Beulah, in what appeared an obvious attempt to impress others at the table, in particular the Diamonds, as to her delicate palate, whined, "Oh, Bill. I can't possibly eat this." It was sent back to the chef. Twice it was sent back. Upon the third delivery of a fresh steak, by her grimace all could see that Beulah still wasn't pleased. Before she was able to complete her pronouncement that the steak still didn't satisfy her, Vi quickly interceded, "Here, Beulah, you take mine. It's perfect!" Beulah was silenced and Vi Diamond ate the steak that hadn't been satisfactory to her. It was only out of a need for decorum that the rest of us at the table didn't stand up and cheer. That was my friend and Joe's wife, Vi Diamond.

It was a year and a half after Vi passed away that well-meaning friends, concerned about Joe living alone, with their little, Cupidesque bows and arrows at the ready, persuaded Joe to begin seeing Ann Dulien, who had been a longtime family friend of the Diamonds. Ann and her husband, Louie, had become very wealthy dealing in scrap metal. One of their business highlights was when they bought the rights to all of the structures on Treasure Island at the conclusion of the World's Fair in 1939. A man-made island, Treasure Island was built specifically for the World's Fair and is attached to Yerba Buena Island roughly halfway to Oakland where the San Francisco Bay bridge touches down for a few moments before going aloft once more on its journey to the east shore of the bay.

Ann had lost her husband earlier, and in January 1981 Ann and Joe were married. With two vast fortunes joining forces, as it were, many of their friends lovingly called it a merger. Together, they built a beautiful home on the shores of Lake Washington. Both had a hand in its design with the help, of course, of a

Ann Dulien Diamond

designer/architect. Gene Detroit, mentioned earlier, was fully involved in the construction of this dream home. Ann and Joe lived in that lovely home until Ann's unfortunate death from cancer, five years to the day after Violett had died. In her memory, Joe built another building at 6 Nickerson Street near Fremont—the Ann Building.

Ann Dulien-Diamond bequeathed one million dollars for a new 30-bed cancer treatment wing on the 12th floor of the Swedish Medical Center in Seattle.

Joe mourned the loss of two beautiful wives to the point that many of his friends, myself included, were concerned for his own health.

Nearly a year and a half later, during a business trip to Chicago, Joe met a remarkable woman, Muriel Bach. Unbeknownst to him at the time, she was a highly respected and much sought-after actress who performed one-woman shows to the delight of audiences over the U.S. and Canada, Muriel and Joe hit it off almost immediately.

SWEDISH

January 1985   SWEDISH HOSPITAL

DULIEN BEQUEST GIVES $1 MILLION FOR CANCER

Ann Dulien Diamond

A $1 million bequest from Ann Dulien Diamond will endow the new 30-bed Ann Dulien Wing for cancer treatment on the twelfth floor of the Southwest Wing, Allan W. Lobb, M.D., medical director, has announced. Mrs. Diamond died here September 4. She was the widow of Louis Dulien of Dulien Steel, Inc., of Seattle and is survived by her husband, Josef Diamond, Seattle attorney.

Her will specified that the bequest is to assist with the construction and furnishing of the twelfth floor and to fund medical research and cancer treatment and be used for any other medical purposes determined by the medical center's Board of Trustees. Her family has said that the bequest was prompted by gratitude to her physician, Saul E. Rivkin, M.D., and to the nursing staff here.

Dr. Lobb said the Dulien Wing, to be dedicated in January, will be the principal general cancer treatment floor of this institution, admitting patients being treated by surgery, chemotherapy and radiation therapy. Bea Lewis, head nurse on 5 North since 1975, will head the staff of the new unit.

The six floors being added to the Southwest Wing will provide space for most of this institution's cancer patients. Two floors will be devoted to those receiving bone marrow transplants under the care of staff of the Fred Hutchinson Cancer Research Center.

Mrs. Diamond's bequest coincides with the medical center's Seventy-fifth Anniversary Year and is a gift comparable in magnitude to several received since the hospital was established.

She tells of those early days, "What was it that drew me to this remarkable man and led me to abandon my home, leave Chicago, and move to Seattle?" She went on, "He was 79 when we began to talk of marriage, and I informed him, 'If we marry, you have to promise me 21 years because when I get married, it is always for 21 years.' Joe paused, looked deep into my eyes and said, 'You're selling me short.'"

Muriel continued her story, "I think what is so exhilarating about being married to a man who is so upbeat is that he makes me feel young—and womanly. The first time I had to leave him for an out-of-town performance, I phoned him from the airport for one last good-bye. He answered the phone in his office, and from the noisy airport phone I whispered, 'I'm just calling to tell you that I love you very much.' There was a momentary pause and he asked, 'Who is this?'"

Muriel continued to perform on stage for many years after their marriage. She played notables from history such as Helen Keller, Eleanor of Aquitaine, and Eleanor Roosevelt. She not only changed costumes onstage in front of her audience as part of the performance, but she also changed countenance. She became the character she was portraying. When she took on her Eleanor Roosevelt character, she became that woman down to and including her prominent front teeth.

Muriel Bach Diamond

During one of Muriel's performances, where Joe had become the de facto stagehand, Lola Hallowell, Muriel's talent agent, asked Joe if he was proud of Muriel. Dumb question. Of course he was proud of her. He answered, "Yes, but if I had known what a great actress she was, I would have been afraid to ask her to marry me. I thought maybe she participated in com-

Monday
November 3, 1986
Bremerton, Wash.

Volume 85, No. 181
25 Cents

The  **Sun**

Diamond's party sparkles in Silverdale

By Ralph Seeley
Sun Staff Writer

Joe Diamond gave a party, and everybody came.

At least, 160 people came. And no wonder. The invitation included a seven-course dinner, entertainment by actress Muriel Bach, overnight accommodations at the new Silverdale Hotel, and brunch Sunday morning.

Also included, if unspoken, was a chance to rub elbows with some of Seattle's wealthiest and most influential people. But that was no big deal, since if you had an invitation, you probably were a wealthy and influential person yourself.

Who is Joe Diamond, you ask? Easily answered.

As mythical a character as Ma Bell, Joe Diamond is best known for his parking lots with barrels that will be chained to your car if you don't pay. But unlike Ma Bell, Joe Diamond actually exists — sort of.

Josef Diamond is a Seattle attorney and real estate magnate who is chairman of the board of the company that owns the Diamond parking lots everyone loves to hate. He is also an owner of the Silverdale Hotel, which explains the location of Saturday's party.

But it's his son, Joel Diamond, who says he broke his father's heart by not going to law school, who is responsible for the verbification of two English nouns — as in "I got barreled" and "I got enveloped." That's how people these days describe their adventures in Diamond lots.

"I'm just a parking lot operator," Joel says. As for being the man responsible for the infamous barrel, he says, "Better that than towing them away and impounding them."

It turns out "parking lot operator" is a

bit of an understatement. The Diamond company buys, improves and rents real estate in 13 states. A lot of that real estate gets turned into parking lots and rented out an hour at a time, it's true. But in Bremerton, for example, a lot of the 25-plus parcels Diamond owns are apartments. Further, Diamond has poured money into refurbishing downtown apartments in the face of criticism from other major property owners in the area.

"(A downtown businessman) told us the money we spent on one place would be completely wasted, that it would just be used for prostitution," Joel said at Saturday's party. "We fixed it up anyway. The occupation rate's been way up, around 95 percent, and there's been no problems with prostitution."

Does he see an upswing in Bremerton's fortunes? "Yes, but it'll be a year or two," he says. He definitely sees new and better things coming, though, "now that the Bremers have, shall we say, been removed from the scene."

ARRIVING AT THE Silverdale Hotel for the party, you half expect to find the parking slots numbered and some barrels sitting around with slogans painted on them: "So sad, you've been bad." But there are no barrels. In fact, it looks more like a parking lot in Beverly Hills than in Silverdale.

Start counting and you get three Porches, five Mercedes Benzes, two Jaguars, one Ferarri and a Rolls Royce that looks as though it just finished the Baja 1000.

That's in the first section. You get no further because an earnest young man appears from the lobby area and asks exactly what you're doing, running around the parking lot taking notes.

Staff photo
Josef Diamond and his wife, actress Muriel Bach, hosting Saturday evening's party in Silverdale.

Inside, the guest list includes a State Supreme Court justice, the former mayor of Bellevue, a Seattle port commissioner, a former King County commissioner, and lots of people whose names you associate with famous Seattle clothing, department or furniture stores.

Also on the list is a former speaker of the state House of Representatives, who gets invited to a lot of Diamond's functions, as well as he should; Jack Sylvester

Please see DIAMOND on B3

munity theater, but then, on our honeymoon, she informed me that she had an engagement in another city to do one of her shows. So, I went with her and got a terrific shock when I saw what a real pro I had on my hands."

5/14/87 Spokane club

CLUB EVENTS continued

OF ALL THE NERVE
performed by Muriel Bach
May Luncheon for Ladies *and* Gentlemen.

Muriel Bach as Maria Montessori

May 14, 1987. Cocktails 11:00, lunch served in the Georgian Room at Noon. Price is $8.40 which includes tax and gratuity. ☎ Reho 838-8511, ext. 239, for reservations.

Muriel Bach, a multifaceted talent, is a character actress of uncanny ability. She carefully researches the histories of the women she portrays, makes them her own, writes and produces the script and, as if by magic, brings those characters to life in their moments of crises. The insightful scenes, fully costumed, intrigue, excite and delight.

Ms. Bach has chosen six women whose lives exhibit daring and determination: Theda Bara, vamp of the silent screen; Maria Montessori, first woman in Italy to become a doctor;

Eleanor of Aquitaine, 12th century Queen of France; Lydia Pinkham, author of the first book on sex education; Gertrude Stein, avant-garde writer and mold-breaker; and Eleanor Roosevelt, humanitarian.

Seeing one woman play six distinct roles allows you to experience those lives. It is all yours for the watching.

205

Muriel continued her comments about life with Joe, "Joe has this incredible capacity to not see evil. I've often wondered how he could be such a successful lawyer. He will not see evil even in his opponents at law. He wants to win the case without seeing the evil. He does not feel any hatred or anger toward people. He is a gentle, gentle man."

ENTERTAINMENT

Bringing characters to life on stage

Actress Muriel Bach brought show to Silverdale with husband Joe Diamond

by Jennie Cooley

Muriel Bach is a risk taker.

She's a risk taker and a professional actress. She recently presented her own special version of one-person theater at a private party hosted by her new husband and part owner of Silverdale Hotel & Resort, Joe Diamond.

Diamond, as in the parking lot Diamonds, hosted his friends to an overnight party at the hotel. It included a Pierre Bittier multi-course dinner and a Sunday brunch.

The story here is not about Diamond, also a risk taker, but it's focus is on his new wife, Muriel Bach, the actress.

Bach's acting career is a very specialized and creative one. She gives a lot of credit to women for helping her career. Her Mother discouraged her from taking a more traditional road to the stage with it's unstable life style, thus forcing her into the challenging and creative "one-person theater."

Bach's daughter encouraged and supported her to create and do her own writing based on her extensive research into the real-life characters she brings to life on stage. She also tired of difficulties with non-acting writers. She said her characters inspire her to reach within, use her skills and training to communicate something the audiences can identify with and take away.

Bach designed and created her own props that she could easily carry and set up herself. Performing before groups from 20 to 2,000 she devised authentic period costumes that could easily be changed and switched onstage. She can quickly change from a young girl in simple dress to a regal royal character while charming audiences during the transition.

Loving color and fabrics, Bach worked with costumers to create dramatic and simple costumes. Theda Bara's dress has golden asps circling the bosom while her Eleanor Roosevelt attire makes audiences look for Falla on the floor.

Over the years Bach created a number of different shows. Each is a series of vignette's about women in conflict. Her playlettes

Bach is married to Joe Diamond, part owner of the Silverdale Hotel.

On a personal note, I would add that I have seen people do Josef dirt, but he seemed to bear no animosity for them. He wouldn't even allow me to express my disgust in his presence for the despicable varmints.

As of this writing, Muriel and Joe have been married 19 years.

Stage performer Muriel Bach.

portray a dramatic moment when faced with crisis the character is forced to resolve a problem or situation.

Last week in Silverdale, she chose moments with Lydia Pinkham, resolving to write a book on sex as a result to letters from customers. Maria Montessori witnessing a child's learning difficulties and Gertrude Stein at a press conference were other characters played by Bach. The actress also played Theda Bara choosing dramatic roles over comedy. Last Saturday, guests in the ballroom also were treated to the Chicago-born Bach's Eleanor Roosevelt indecision in accepting her United Nations appointment and then there was Eleanor of Aquitaine planting a "seed" in her priest's mind to grant her an annulment from Louis VII and arranging a marriage to Henry II of England.

The great closing line written by Bach for Eleanor goes something like this: "A woman gets what she wants, the queen would have said, by using her body . . . especially her head."

Bach may consider civil rights leader Rosa Parks in a future show but at this time is not interested in creating a new show.

"I've got a whole new marriage and a whole new life here in Seattle," she stated. "That's so time consuming and you really have to push everything out of your life to do that [create a new show]. I'm not willing to do that right now."

Overcoming stage fright was another risk for Bach even after extensive theater training with Drama Coach Alvina Krause. She's also earned a drama degree from Northwestern University.

One-person theater is so unique and creative that actress Bach finally unlocked the key to this dilemma by concentrating on the material and not the audience.

Muriel Bach might remind a theater-goer of the elegant "Mary Martin," matching her enthusiam and energy during a performance. She has been inspired by others in the specialized art form such as Hal Holbrook and James Whitmore

Bach's success is no surprise she stresses the importance of being well physically, not just feeling good, but feeling great. Bach said she draws her strength from her characters, believing them worthy, insightful and inspiring.

Muriel Bach believes in what she is doing and it shows.

MEMORIES

Merle Dulien (Ann Dulien-Diamond's daughter) tells: "I found an unfamiliar stuffed animal in our family apartment in Los Angeles. It was white and black and fuzzy. It may have been a Snoopy. My mother told me Joe had given it to her. I was really touched by such a romantic gesture and the tenderness it implied between two mature adults. I would have loved Joe for that even if I hadn't met him."

"The best thing that Joe Diamond has done for both of us is bring Muriel Bach Diamond into our lives. She, too, is magic, special, and wonderful, and we feel we have been enriched beyond our dreams for having these two wonderful people among our friends.

"We wish them both nothing but joy and happiness and a long life together."

— Shirley Fleischmann

Gary Glant adds to Joe's Book of Memories: "A few years back at a dinner party my parents, Earle and Evie Glant, had for visiting Chicago friends, Horty and the late Leo Singer, Leo turned to Joe and said, 'Have I got a girl for you!' The 'girl' turned out to be beautiful, talented Muriel."

"It is a great pleasure to honor you on your 83rd birthday. Your 'Book of Memories' must be a very full one because of the very full life you have led.

"You have been a longtime supporter of Swedish. Your support of the hospital has been great, particularly shown by the generosity of you and Mrs. Diamond (Ann Dulien) in the development of the Ann Dulien Cancer Care Unit.

"We thank you and hope you have another healthy 83 years."
> – Brian W. Goodell, M.D.
> Executive Director of Swedish Hospital Medical Center

"I married Edward Stern almost 55 years ago. Among his friends was a most attractive couple, Vi and Joe Diamond, whom I recall seeing on a number of occasions."
> – Bernice Stern

Susan Wolfson (Muriel's daughter) added: "When I first met Joe Diamond four years ago, he put his best foot forward and so did I. He told his best stories and did his very best to impress me with what a nice guy he was. I expected that. He was in love with my mother. My mother was in love with him, and Joe wanted my approval.

"What impressed me more, however, was the string of people I have met in the last four years who share the view of what a fine fellow this Josef Diamond really is. Man after man has told his story of how Joe Diamond set him up in business, saved his business, loaned him the money to start his business, gave him invaluable advice that guaranteed the success of his business, invested in his business, or simply befriended him and changed his life. Joe has been the key factor in changing the destiny of so many whose lives touched his. He has the unceasing love and respect of so many people whose lives have crossed his path.

"My mom loves Joe. She's bound to think he's terrific. It is the long list of friends and business associates who regularly validate what a great guy this Joe Diamond really is."

[Sadly, Susan died not long ago at the age of 54.]

Josef Diamond, Lawyer

CHAPTER TWENTY ONE
HERE COMES THE JUDGE

For the March 2002 issue of the King County Bar Association publication, the *Bar Bulletin*, a profile of Joe Diamond was written by Washington State Supreme Court Justice Tom Chambers:

When I reported to work that first day in the summer of 1969, I had a plan. The secret to get ahead, I thought, was to be the first one in the office in the morning and the last one to leave at night. My plan had a problem. The problem was Josef Diamond. He started to work about 8:00

My Plan Had a Problem.
The Problem Was Josef Diamond.

(Credit: *Bar Bulletin*, March 2002)

in the morning and would leave the law office about 8:00 at night. On the way out he would say good night to me. He was on his way to work another shift at the parking lot office.

As a kid, I eagerly awaited the arrival of the *Reader's Digest* so I could read the monthly installment of "The Most Unforgettable Character I Ever Met." You may think of Joe Diamond as the son of a tailor who built a financial empire, but to me he is the most unforgettable character I ever met.

Sure, he scared me at first. Why not? He was a big man with an imposing presence and booming voice. But I quickly learned that he was not only one of the state's most dynamic, creative, and resourceful lawyers, but he was also a very thoughtful caring man. He never raised his voice and he never swore. He had created a powerful law firm in Lycette, Diamond and Sylvester. Joe was a great trial lawyer, Lyle Iverson was an outstanding appellate lawyer, and if they both failed, Jack Sylvester, who at age 29 had been the youngest Speaker of the House in the state legislature, would go to Olympia and change the law. Then there was Simon Wampold, who represented banks; Al Prince, who represented surety companies; and—well I guess you get the drift.

Joe was the rainmaker. He represented 90 percent of the construction firms in the city as well as the

Associated General Contractors, Seattle Construction Council, Seattle Master Builders and Home Builders. Every time he would come back from a meeting he would bring with him four or five new cases.

"A Lawsuit Is Like a War"

I learned much about trial work in the two years that I worked for Joe. Once I had agreed to continue a motion, and since the other lawyer had requested the continuance, he had agreed to notify the court. "Never," bellowed Joe when he heard. "Never allow another lawyer to take control of your case—even scheduling a motion." "A lawsuit is like a war," he taught me. I heard many military metaphors: always gather "intelligence," take the "initiative," occupy from

Special Award of Honor

FIFTY-YEAR LAWYERS . . . Honored at the 1981 Annual Business Meeting for completing fifty years' service as members of the Washington State Bar Association were (l. to r.) Josef Diamond, John W. Dobson, Thomas L. Morrow, Judge Frank W. Ryan, and Carl H. Skoog. Also cited, but not available to be photographed, were Robert D. Campbell, J. Kennard Cheadle, Van R. Hinkle, Byron E. Lutterman, Oliver Malm, George W. Martin, F.P. Mason, Edgar E. Neal, John Panesko, Sr., DeForest Perkins, Judge Warner Poyhonen, C.C. Quackenbush, Felix Rea, DeWitt C. Rowland, Frank J. Ruff, and Patrick Henry Winston.

"high ground," and so forth. "Never rely on anyone else to do anything," he said, "every act requires a follow-up." He taught me a simple tickler system that required a follow-up deadline for every letter and pleading. It is far superior to anything the software industry has ever developed.

Joe Diamond is a great and gifted lawyer. Shortly before I joined the firm he had obtained a jury verdict against the city of Seattle in the sum of $4.5 million dollars—a mind-boggling sum in the sixties. The city had issued a building permit to build the Roanoke Reef Apartments 20 feet above Lake Union. After construction began, the city canceled the permit. It was a landmark case shortly after the repeal of sovereign immunity.

Among his many notable cases, famous to some and infamous to others, is the DeFunis case. Joe took the case to the United States Supreme Court to establish that reverse discrimination was unconstitutional. DeFunis, a young married man, had graduated from the University of Washington Phi Beta Kappa with a 3.9 grade average. He had applied to the university's law school the previous year and had been rejected despite his almost perfect grades. He was told to apply the next year, and when he was turned down the second year, he sought Diamond's help. Pretrial discovery revealed that some of the students admitted instead of DeFunis had grade point averages of 2.5, and one file had an entry "don't believe she is qualified or will make it, but admit." In September 1971, Joe got a restraining order from Judge Howard Thompson to stop the university from mailing out acceptances to any law student until the DeFunis problem was solved. Joe struck a deal with the university that it could admit the remaining students if DeFunis was permitted to attend class pending the outcome of the case. Judge Lloyd Shorett ruled in DeFunis's favor. The State Supreme Court reversed and Diamond appealed, taking the case to the United State Supreme Court, where he and Attorney General Slade Gorton argued. The United States Supreme Court reversed the Washington State Supreme Court and Marco DeFunis obtained his JD.

As a fighter for individual rights, he also took on the Harbor Club. Once an all-male club, Joe thought it was unfair to women and helped convince the Harbor Club to let women join.

I Was Not Surprised to Find Him Still Working

Leaving Lycette, Diamond and Sylvester was inevitable for me, but I left after only two years. Leaving so soon was a career mistake because I was learning so much and was treated so well. Joe and I have stayed in touch over the years, having lunch together occasionally. He is now 95 years young, but I was not surprised to find him still working at the parking lot office at the

Diamond Building. He still has his impressive presence and booming voice, although now he prefers that I speak a little louder.

All Big Deals Cross His Desk

The *Seattle Post-Intelligencer* once said, "Any large real estate deal in downtown Seattle probably ends up on Joe's desk." Joe Diamond has had a remarkable impact on the face and soul of Seattle. We have all heard of Diamond Parking.

Interestingly, the United States Army may have given Diamond a great start in real estate. In 1941, as World War II spread, Joe was called to active duty in the Judge Advocate's Corps at Camp Murray. He quickly rose through the ranks to become Colonel Diamond, working in Washington, D.C., in the Judge Advocate General's department. Much of his work involved acquiring property for airports, including ones in Moses Lake and Tacoma. He swapped property for contract cancellations with the Ford Motor Company, and in another instance paid a contractor two million dollars over his bid to get an airfield completed during the war. He became a troubleshooter and problem solver for the Army and was given the Legion of Merit medal for his contributions.

When he came back from the war he took over the parking business his brother had started. There were four lots, but under Joe's guidance the business has grown to over 1,000 lots and garages in nine states. I do not know the size of the Diamond empire. I have never asked and Joe has never volunteered. The bits and pieces I do know are enough for me. When I worked for him, in 1970, he owned the Budget Rental Car franchises for Washington and Oregon. He owned franchises for Fisk Batteries and Siberling Tires. He co-owned Gov-Mart—an early version of Costco. He helped found and was a director of Northwest Bank, which merged with Old National Bank, and then Peoples Bank, which was acquired by U.S. Bank. Thirty years later his business empire, which includes hotels, literally spans the world.

You Made Infinitely More Money in Business, So Why Have You Practiced Law for More Than 70 Years?

Paul Cressman, Sr., made an interesting point. "Joe Diamond is a great and remarkable lawyer for many reasons. What always struck me was that he could have and undoubtedly did make infinitely more money in business, but he chose to be a full-time lawyer. I finally decided that the law and Joe were a perfect fit. His avocation was his vocation."

Craig Sternberg, a contemporary of mine, had another insight. "Joe only had one word on his business card and that was 'lawyer,' not 'counsellor,' or 'attorney at law,' just lawyer. Joe thinks that it is a great honor to be a lawyer. He took cases without regard to pay. The DeFunis case was pro bono and many of his cases were pro bono. He used to say to me, 'Don't worry about the money, just take care of your clients. If you take care of your clients, first respect will come and then the money will come.' I don't know any lawyer who enjoys more respect from his clients than Joe Diamond."

I finished my interview with Joe Diamond with this question, "Joe, you made infinitely more money in business, so why have you practiced law for more than 70 years?" Joe smiled; I could tell that I had asked him an easy question. "People come to you with their problems. I like to help people and I like to solve problems. When you help people solve their problems it is very rewarding. That reward is more important to me than money." Then his smile grew broader and his eyes twinkled, "Besides, I learned a lot from the mistakes that my clients made and I didn't make the same mistakes."

When the Rest of Us Are Running from Difficulty— He Is Looking for Opportunity

I have learned much from Joe Diamond, more than just a 12-hour workday, and to me he will always be unforgettable. He is a brilliant lawyer and an astute business person—an uncommon combination. He applies his unique common sense to the practice of law and settles costly cases quickly. He always keeps his eye on the big picture and is never distracted. When the rest of us are running from difficulty, he is looking for opportunity. One of six children, raised on the earnings of a tailor, Joe Diamond sought, seized, and has lived the American Dream.

Washington Supreme Court Justice Tom Chambers was elected in 2000 after a distinguished 30-year legal career. Justice Chambers served as president of the Washington State Bar Association, the Washington State Trial Lawyers Association, the Washington Chapter of American Board of Trial Advocates, and the Damages Attorney Round Table. He served on the Board of Governors for the American Trial Lawyers Association. He also employed *Bar Bulletin* editor Bob Anderton, hence his willingness to write this profile notwithstanding other responsibilities.

MEMORIES

"I think we first met at the King County Courthouse over 50 years ago when you were giving a violin lesson to some hapless young attorney in Judge Malcolm Douglas's courtroom. Bob Graham and I were awaiting our turn on the motion calendar.

"While I still pay my dues to the Bar Association, I was never able to both practice law and rent out cars and provide places for them as well as the rest of us to park. The most I could do at Bogle's was to usher at

night at the old Metropolitan Theatre when the stage plays and musicals came through town—after which Jack Baird and I would go to Manca's on Columbia for some razor clam hash.

"Ruth and I watch with interest as you pursue the law so feverishly after most of your former partners have left for the cosmos. We believe that you and Muriel have a great future ahead and cherish your friendship.

"May you long continue to flourish."

– Robert B. Dunn
Chairman of King County Council

Seattle Loses Roanoke Reef Suit

BY MARIBETH MORRIS

A Superior Court jury decided yesterday that the City of Seattle owes the developers of the planned Roanoke Reef condominium on Lake Union just under $2.9 million because the city halted the construction shortly after work was started.

City taxpayers may wind up paying the bill because Signal Insurance Co., the city's insurance carrier, has maintained it is not liable for any damages resulting from the suit filed by Roanoke Reef developers.

But John Harris, city corporation counsel, said the judgment will be appealed, directly to the State Supreme Court if possible.

The jury voted unanimously that the city should pay the developers $2,896,534 for financial loss suffered after construction was begun in 1970. The city had issued a building permit for the $5.3-million condominium, but the permit was invalidated by the State Supreme Court in July, 1973.

Federal court records show that after the Roanoke Reef damage suit asking $3 million was filed, Signal Insurance Co. sued the city asking that U.S. District Court Judge Morell Sharp rule the insurance company not liable for any damages which might result from the litigation.

Sharp refused to make a decision either way pending outcome of the damage suit. Now the question of Signal's liability may again end up before Sharp.

If the city ultimately loses an appeal, it will have to not only pay the $2.9 million but 8 per cent interest per annum on the judgment as well.

An appeal direct to the Supreme Court, circumventing the State Court of Appeals, could cut the time lag down.

Meanwhile yesterday, Roanoke Reef developers Fred Haslund, Jack Samuelson and Carl Schaber who brought the lawsuit were elated over the jury's verdict.

"We're delighted. The jury was made up of people like you and me who believed we got a bad deal," Schaber said.

Joe Diamond, who along with his partner, Robert Ratcliffe, served as attorney for the developers during the past five years of fighting environmentalists and neighborhood groups in the court and City Council chambers, said:

"It was a lot of money for the jury (to award). But it was a very fair and very fine verdict."

The developers still own the Lake Union property, which now includes a mammoth concrete and steel over-the-water platform.

The slab was to have served as the foundation for the five-story condominium.

That was the construction stage when the Supreme Court ruled the building permit was invalid because city building code procedures in issuing the permit were invalid.

The court also held an environmental-impact statement should have been prepared because of a law that went into effect after the building permit for Roanoke Reef was issued but before a renewal for the permit was granted.

The developers claim they can't do anything with the property now that the slab is on it extending out into the water; that it would cost $500,000 to tear the slab down.

Diamond said the property without the slab has been appraised at $330,000; with the slab, $153,000.

"It's been up for sale for a long time now," Diamond said. "Maybe, the city could buy it for a park."

CHAPTER TWENTY TWO
AND NOW . . .

We're five years into the new century, and the Diamond dynasty and legacy continues.

Joe Diamond, having passed his 98th birthday, continues to practice law, goes to his office on the second floor of the Diamond building almost every day, and remains a strong influence over the many business ventures he has been or is involved in. He is still sought out for business advice by the many who have relied upon his input for so many years.

His practice of law is pretty much confined to looking after his own affairs now, but knowing him, I suspect he'd jump into the legal fray if one of his hundreds of close friends were in need.

Diamond Parking continues to grow under the guidance of its current president and chief operating officer, Jonathon (Jon) Diamond, Joe's very capable grandson. Joe's son, Joel, like his father, continues to be intimately involved in the overall

Josef, Joel, and Jon Diamond

Diamond Parking entity, including its many properties and other holdings, but interferes very little with Jon as far as day-to-day happenings are concerned.

Budget Rent A Car of Washington-Oregon, Inc., was sold out to the home corporation (some of us think, unfortunately) back in 1988, but Joe continued in an advisory capacity until just very recently. From a personal standpoint, I can't help but mention that I feel strongly that Budget was being run much more efficiently and profitably when we were the franchisees, but I suppose that could be just a matter of personal pride.

I do know that it was a sad day when I noted that Budget no longer operated the large parking lot across Highway 99 (International Boulevard) from SeaTac airport with its massive "green monstrosity" billboard. It was one of our more important profit centers when we were in the saddle.

On the bright side, I'm pleased to see more and more Budget rental trucks on the road. We in Washington and Oregon were one of the bigger proponents of Budget getting heavily into the truck rental business both for local rentals as well as one-way rentals from one city to another, and Joe Diamond championed that proposal for many years.

We lost Johnny Cain nearly 20 years ago. The man that Jules Lederer thought was too old for the job was a sparkplug right up to his last breath. He and I had kind of a love-hate relationship. Each of us, more than once, offered to pour a pint of Irish whiskey on the other's grave. It was one of those "If you don't mind if I pass it through me kidneys first" type of commitments. But, he outsmarted me. He arranged for his remains to be interred in a niche high up on the wall, knowing well that I couldn't reach him. I'm sure he went to his grave chuckling.

Muriel and Joe enjoy living in a beautiful, seventh-floor condominium on top of Queen Anne Hill, overlooking Seattle,

Billboards in Seattle on Joe Diamond's 95th birthday

Diamond's long career has been labor of love

By MARC STILES
Journal Real Estate Editor

He helped start what today is the world's oldest parking company.

His fierce drive is so well known that it has been mentioned in Ann Landers' column.

Diamond

And at 92, Joe Diamond, the oldest practicing lawyer in Washington state, shows few signs of letting up.

Naturally, Diamond, the son of Russian immigrants, has countless tales to tell and he's patient enough to recount many of them. Yet so voluminous is his history, that he's at a loss to explain just how he got going in real estate.

He looks out the window of his 30th floor office of the Well Fargo Tower in downtown Seattle. There's a long pause. "Well, I don't know where to start," he says humbly.

Diamond's resume is long and impressive. Law partner at Diamond & Sylvester for 49 years. Chairman of the boards of Diamond Parking, Washington Mortgage and other businesses. President of Madison Properties and Vine Investment Corp. Director of eight other enterprises and partner in 15 more.

He also has been a fighter for equal rights. Consider that he convinced the once all-male Harbor Club to let women join. Pragmatism prompted him to act. Marilyn Harlan, then an executive with the parking company, was unable to attend functions at the club, and Diamond didn't think that was right.

He began building his list of accomplishments at a time when the odds were stacked against everyone. The world was stuck in the throes of the Great Depression when he graduated from the University of Washington's School of Law. Each day, Diamond walked through the office buildings in downtown Seattle seeking work at one of the law firms.

"I got turned down by every one of 'em," he recalled. It looked as though he would have to break his mother's heart by joining the Navy. At the last minute, he convinced one firm, Caldwell Lycette, to let him work for free for 30 days.

As Ann Landers noted in a column 13 years ago, Diamond was the first to arrive for work and last to leave. He worked weekends. After a month, the firm wouldn't let him leave. Four years later he was made a partner.

Diamond, however, is not known

(Continued on Page 6, Column 1)

226

Elliott Bay, Puget Sound, West Seattle, and points west, including the southern reaches of the Olympic Mountain range. The scene of the ferries wending their way across the water is nothing short of a living picture postcard. From the Diamonds' living room or dining room, one can almost see the corner of Westlake and Virginia, where our first Budget Rent A Car office was located. As of this writing, that office still exists. When darkness falls over Seattle and the lights come on, the Emerald City twinkles like the gem that it is, especially if the streets are wet from rain.

Muriel and Joe are still, after these many years, very much in love, and they spend as much time as is possible together. Muriel keeps a watchful eye on the old McDonald's hamburger lover's diet and encourages him to exercise regularly, though all the while catering (she lets him think that) to his every wish.

Seattle has gone from being a one-horse and two-car town to being one of the most important business centers in the country, with traffic congestion that would make Los Angeles freeways seem like a country road. The Smith Tower, which at one time was the tallest building in the world outside of New York, with its 28 stories, once dominated the Seattle skyline. Today it is dwarfed and almost hidden by the many skyscrapers surrounding it.

At one time, Seattle was pretty much a one-industry city. When Boeing had a problem, everyone suffered. In late 1960 and early 1970, Boeing came on hard times and dropped from

Diamond buys 46% of warehouse

By JOE NABBEFELD

July Journal Real Estate Editor

Dec 10 2002

A Martin Smith partnership sold nearly half of a warehouse building south of Boeing Field to parking magnate Joe Diamond for $4.5 million because Diamond requested a place to reinvest proceeds from a $5.5 million Kirkland apartment sale.

The selling partnership includes former Tully's Coffee CEO Jamie Colbourne and principals of the Seattle real estate investment and development firm of Martin Smith Inc.

King County property records show the partnership received $4.525 million from Diamond's Westwood Square Associates LLC late last week in a deal involving the 124,000-square-foot former Seattle Packaging warehouse at 3701 S. Norfolk St.

Diamond said in a short telephone interview that he bought only a portion of the property. The Martin Smith group paid $8.3 million a little more than two years ago and a broker had asked $9 million for last summer.

"Joe called a couple of months ago and said 'I'm selling a property, do you have something we can trade into?' " said Mickey Smith, lead Martin Smith Inc. principal in the Norfolk Street property. "We thought about it and decided to sell him 46 percent."

Reinvesting proceeds from commercial real estate sales via 1031 exchanges allows deferring payment of substantial taxes.

Colbourne and the other principals remain in the partnership, Smith said.

Property records show that in October, Diamond and one-time Cornerstone Columbia Development Co. head Bill Weisfield sold the Westwood Village apartments on Northeast 138th Place in the north end of Kirkland for $5.5 million. The buyer was Westwood Village LLC.

When the Martin Smith partnership bought the Norfolk Street warehouse, Mickey Smith said the possibility of converting it to a data center contributed to making the purchase but wasn't the sole driving factor.

Shortly after that purchase, the data center fever cooled off.

Speculators had bought warehouse properties at inflated prices on the hope of converting them to lucrative data centers. After the dot-com and telecom bubble burst, many speculators ended up taking big hits as they either released the space at warehouse rates or sold at big losses.

Martin Smith didn't convert the property to a data center, but it also isn't taking a hit on the deal, Mickey Smith said, because "it's fully leased."

When it bought, Martin Smith had an intended user that it expected would sign a lease, but that came apart, Smith said. Seattle Packaging, meanwhile, sold because it planned to move to Kent Valley.

By this summer, Colliers International broker Wilma Warshak had located four new tenants: the mechanical and electrical contractor Encompass, which took about half; Masin's Furniture; the game company Front Porch Classics; and TelWest Communications, which took the structure's 12,000 square feet of offices.

The $4.5 million price for 46 percent indicates the owners place a $9.8 million value on the full property, which Smith described as high quality, in part because Seattle Packaging had built it for itself. The price Diamond paid equals $79 per square foot.

On a notice marketing the space for lease last July, Warshak added that the building could also be bought, with a $9 million asking price. Smith said that wasn't a formal offering and the building was never up for sale.

Diamond, who is in his 80s, has invested in real estate with the Smith family for decades, going back years with Martin Smith Inc. founder Martin Smith Jr., Mickey Smith's father. Diamond said he never even looked at the Norfolk Street property, but rather just asked the Smiths to put him in the right deal and went with what they recommended.

Joe Nabbefeld can be reached at (206) 219-6518 or by e-mail at joe@djc.com.

228

something over 100,000 employees in the area down to, as I recall, 35,000 almost overnight. There was a large billboard on Highway 99 south of town with the words, "Will the last person leaving Seattle turn out the lights?"

Those days are no longer. While Boeing is an important part of the Puget Sound area, many industries have made western Washington their home. One such, of which everyone on earth has become aware, is Bill Gates's Microsoft, with its headquarters just across Lake Washington from Seattle.

It may be worth mentioning that Bill Gates, when he was a much younger and not nearly as wealthy man, bought Joe Diamond's home in Laurelhurst with frontage on Lake Washington. Joe tells that story these days with a certain tone of pride in his voice.

Joe is, as he has always been, a tenderhearted and gentle man. He continues to be more concerned about the welfare of his friends than he seems to be about his own. If he knows of someone in need, he offers help without a moments hesitation.

He is also a very private man. What contributions or help-ing hands he has made to the various charities are for his knowledge and his alone. He has no wish to impress others with his philanthropy. While he cares about others, I don't believe he cares a *whit* about what the media thinks of his philanthropic bestowals.

But to those who know him intimately and to those for whom he cares, his quickness to help is no secret. I have personally watched him prop people up in times of need regardless of the number of dollars involved. His only qualification for such assistance would depend upon his belief that the help was truly needed.

That is the Joe Diamond I know.

ABOUT THE AUTHOR

John Pierre is a decorated United States Navy veteran of the Korean War, having served on the flight deck of two aircraft carriers, the USS *Bataan*, CVL-29, and the USS *Kearsarge*, CVA-33, as an ordnanceman (the person who services and loads the 20 mm wing cannons, and loads and fuses the bombs, rockets, and torpedoes). He served as "ship's company" on the *Kearsarge* and later on that same vessel with Attack Squadron 115 made up of AD-1 Skyraiders. ADs were the planes that took out the bridges at Toko Ri (a fictional place representing some real bridges and a series of real attacks in Korea), not the jet aircraft as depicted in the James Michener story and movie of that title.

He is past president of CATRALA of Washington (Car and Truck Rental and Leasing Association) and past president of the Association for Retarded Citizens of Snohomish County, Washington. He is a member of the Edmonds Police Foundation (a nonprofit organization made up of private citizens dedicated to raising money for the purpose of providing funding to the Edmonds Police Department for needed items not covered for in their limited budget), and among his duties there is public relations between that group and the media.

A prolific op-ed writer for local newspapers, John Pierre is editor and producer of monthly in-house publications for Thrifty Car Rental, Huling Bros. Auto Center, and previously for Budget Rent A Car. Combined, he has written in that capacity for more than 25 years. He is happiest when writing humor.

He and his wife are parents of three, grandparents of seven, and great-grandparents of six. Rosie, his high school sweetheart, who became his wife while he was in the navy in 1952, when he was 18 and she was 19, and he have been married over 52 years.

– Tom D. Huling III
Partner in Huling Bros.
Auto Center and Operating
Partner of Thrifty Car
Rental, Seattle, Bellevue,
Portland and Beaverton, OR